**Donnelly**

*Pierre Gibault, Missionary, 1737-1802*

by Joseph P. Donnelly, S.J.

Cloth, viii + 199 pages, 1971
$8.00 T
ISBN 0-8294-0203-9
Library of Congress catalog card number: 77-156371

In spite of his valuable contribution to the success of George Rogers Clark's invasion of the Mississippi Valley during our Revolution, Pierre Gibault has never been the subject of a full-length biography until now. Gibault supported our effort for independence in direct opposition to his ecclesiastical superior, the bishop of Quebec. He lived through the difficult years of transition from French dominion over the Mississippi Valley, through Spanish control, and finally, dominion by the United States. A much misunderstood figure in his own day, his help to our national beginnings was a noteworthy contribution never before fully outlined and carefully documented.

Monseigneur

1 avril 1783.

Je n'ay une demie-heure pour profiter de l'occasion De Mr. Du Charme, Je ne puis Dans ce
court interval Marquer à Votre Grandeur
sinon que Je suis toujours le même pour le
salut des peuples, excepté que l'age et Les fatigues
ne me permettent plus de faire ce que Je Desire-
vois, Comme autrefois. le R. pere Bernard
Capucin, Dessert les Kahokias Conjointement
avec St. Louis ou il Demeure, ce qui me soulage
Du plus éloigné village que J'aye a Desservir.
Les Illinois sont plus malheureux qu'ils n'ont
jamais été. après avoir été Ruinés et Epuisés
par Les Virginiens, Laissés sans Commendant
sans troupes et sans Justice, ils se gouvernent
eux mêmes par fantaisie et Caprice, ou pour
mieu Dire par la loy Du plus fort.

nous attendons cependant en peu de tems des
troupes avec un Commendant et une justice Reglé
J'espere faire un Detail le mieux qu'il me sera
possible a Votre Grandeur, par Mr Dubue qui
Reste encore quelque tems, De tout ce qui s'est
passé Depuis quatre ou Cinq ans. J'espere aussi
De Votre Charité paternel que Vous ne me Lais
serez pas non plus sans Consolation, J'en plus
Besoin que jamais quoyque j'aye prir pour
principe de faire tout ce que je fais comme je
le ferais en presence de mon Evêque Et que
par Consequent Vous Etes toujours present à mes
yeux Et a mon Esprit, il me serait bien Doux
De Recevoir Vos instructions en attendant ce bon
heur J'estois avec tout Le Respect La Soumission
Et Lobeissance La plus parfaite

a Ste Genevieve
Le 1er avril            Votre très humble Serviteur
1783.                        P. Gibault, Prêtre.

---

*The original is preserved in the archives of the Archdiocese of Quebec where it is identified as E.U., VI, 48.*

April 1, 1783.

Monseigneur:

I have only a half an hour, if I seize the opportunity of sending a letter afforded me by Mr. Ducharme. In this short space I can only point out to your Lordship that I am always the same in working for the salvation of the people, except that age and weariness do not permit me as formerly to do what I would desire. The Reverend Father Bernard, Capuchin, serves the people of Cahokia, as well as those of St. Louis where he lives. The Illinois people are more unfortunate than they were. After having been ruined and worn out by the Virginians and left without a commandant, without troops, and without justice, they are governing themselves by whim and caprice, or, to put it better, by the law of the strongest. We are expecting, however, in a short time, some troops with a commandant and a regulated court of justice. I hope to send your Lordship by Mr. Dubuque who still remains here some time, a detailed account, as far as I can, of all that has occurred within the last four or five years. I trust, likewise, that through your paternal charity, you will not leave me longer without consolation. I have more need of it than ever, though I have made it a principle to perform all my duties as if they were done in the presence of my Bishop; and since, consequently, you are always present to my eyes and to my spirit, it would be very agreeable to me to receive your instructions. While waiting for that good fortune, I am, with all respect, submission, and the most perfect obedience,

Your very humble servant,
P. Gibault, Priest.

At Ste. Genevieve
April 1, 1783.

JOSEPH P. DONNELLY, s.j.

# Pierre Gibault, Missionary 1737-1802

LOYOLA UNIVERSITY PRESS

*Chicago, Illinois* 60657

© 1971 Loyola University Press

Printed in the United States of America
Library of Congress Catalog Card Number: 77-156371
ISBN 0-8294-0203-9

*About this book*

*Pierre Gibault, Missionary, 1737-1802* was set in the composing room of
Loyola University Press. The text is 12/14 Bodoni Book; the reduced matter,
10/12; the notes, 8/10. The display type is 12 Bodoni Book caps.

It was printed by Photopress, Inc., on Warren's 60-pound English Finish
paper and bound by The Engdahl Company in Bancroft cloth.

# CONTENTS

I

---

PIERRE GIBAULT,

AN HISTORICAL ENIGMA

With the approach of the bicentenary of the American Revolution, a great flood of historical literature concerning every phase of that momentous event will pour forth from publishing houses. Among the studies rightly to be expected will probably be a series of monographs on, if not a new biography of, George Rogers Clark, emphasizing the importance of his daring invasion of the Mississippi Valley in 1778. Inevitably, Father Pierre Gibault's name will again come to the fore, if only because of his part in Clark's operation. While the key incidents in Gibault's life certainly were his relationship to Clark at Kaskaskia and his part, if any, in persuading the citizens of Vincennes to take an oath of allegiance to the American cause, the missionary's whole active life was one long series of puzzling conflicts.

Because it is presently impossible to learn anything about Pierre Gibault's childhood and early education, one is at a loss to surmise what sort of a man he was likely to have become. As a stripling, was he an *engagé* of one or other fur trader with whom he came to the Illinois Country among the roistering voyageurs? Or was he brought there as a small child by his parents who very soon returned with him to Canada? If the first be correct, the fact might explain why Gibault, as a grown man, was an eager participant in outdoor sports with the younger element of his parishioners. If the second, it is much easier to understand how he possessed sufficient academic training permitting him to enter the seminary at the quite advanced age of about twenty-eight, a time of life when most of his contemporaries were married and the heads of families.

From the very beginning of Gibault's ecclesiastical career, he was looked upon with some distrust by his superiors. Jean-Olivier Briand, the bishop of Quebec who conferred priestly ordination on Gibault, sent the new priest to the Illinois Country with many misgivings. For approximately three years after settling at Kaskaskia, Gibault was enthusiastically welcomed by the people. But from the beginning, this pastor was something of a "new breed" for the people. They had never seen a missionary set out on a sacerdotal excursion with a brace of pistols strapped to his waist nor had they encountered one who loved to hunt and fish. Certainly they had no contact with a priest who was said, perhaps unfairly, to boast of his capacity for eau-de-vie. Withal, Gibault was a zealous pastor who did not spare himself for the spiritual welfare of his people. In 1775, after a flying visit to Canada, Gibault began to express disillusionment regarding his mission in the Illinois Country. His critics among the people, he felt, were grossly unjust. What was far more diffi-

2

cult for him to bear, his bishop appeared too inclined to con-
demn him unheard.

By 1778, when Gibault had fairly well resigned himself to
criticism, he became involved with General Clark's invasion of
the Mississippi Valley. There are, perhaps, as many opinions
about the missionary's part in that important operation as there
are historians who have written about it. Clark, himself, portrayed Gibault as something quite close to a sniveling coward.
However, Patrick Henry, then governor of Virginia, wrote glow-
ingly to Clark concerning the priest's valiant aid and charged
the general to thank Gibault in the name of Virginia. Henry
Hamilton, the British commander who recaptured Vincennes
after the citizens there had forsworn allegiance to George III,
wrote that he considered Gibault to be a particularly daring,
dangerous, and influential man who should be hanged. Jacob P.
Dunn, whose study of Gibault appeared in 1905, flatly maintained that the priest was the outstanding patriot of the Old
Northwest without whose aid and advice Clark's effort would
have been a dismal failure. Clarence W. Alvord, writing in
1922, paints a picture of the missionary which is anything but
attractive, though he readily admits that Gibault was a zealous
priest. Which of these many opinions shows us the real Gibault?

Two years after Clark's conquest, Pierre Gibault was seriously censured by his bishop who imposed on him the ecclesiastical penalty of suspension. This drastic action, issued on June
12, 1780, should indicate some grave moral fault of which the
missionary was, supposedly, guilty in some public manner.
Strangely, the suspension, by the bishop's own declaration, did
not forbid Gibault to exercise at least some sacerdotal functions,
though the penalty, by the strictest norms of ecclesiastical law,
should have forbidden the culprit to say Mass or administer any
of the sacraments, except to persons in grave danger of death
when no other priest was available. Also, Briand's document
should have clearly stated the cause for which the censure was

imposed. But nothing in the communication gives any hint of the reason. Apparently Father Gibault either did not receive the bishop's letter or he simply ignored it. There is nothing in the baptismal or other records of the parishes he was then serving to indicate that he did not continue his priestly ministrations unabated. Nevertheless, the fact of the suspension was known to the laity who used it as an argument to the Congress in a petition seeking to prevent the missionary from being granted land.

When the American colonies revolted against England, Bishop Briand went to great lengths to prevent his flock from joining forces with their American neighbors. Briand argued that since the French had, in good faith, taken an oath of allegiance to the British crown, they were morally bound to honor that pledge and would, thus, be guilty of serious moral fault if they aided the Americans. Those who did not heed the directive of their bishop were visited with the severest of ecclesiastical penalties. Many of the laity who helped the Americans were excommunicated, as were some few priests who showed sympathy for the revolting Americans. If Father Gibault had ever admitted to his bishop that he had formally accepted American citizenship, perhaps ecclesiastical suspension might be explained, even though, according to ecclesiastical law, Briand would have been hard put to it to prove that he could actually suspend anyone on the grounds of political allegiance alone. But, compounding confusion, Gibault flatly denied aiding the American cause in any manner, at least so he protested to his bishop. However, the missionary, by turns, actually protested undying loyalty to George III and eternal gratitude to the Americans for bringing the blessings of liberty to himself and his people. While Father Gibault might have been able to reconcile these diametrically opposed positions in his own mind, his statements on the matter present no small mystery.

From 1780 forward, Pierre Gibault received little consideration at the hands of the bishop of Quebec and, later, from

John Carroll who became bishop of Baltimore. When Gibault pleaded with Quebec's bishop to allow him to return to Canada, he was most coldly rebuffed. When he asked to join Carroll's newly erected diocese, that prelate firmly refused to accept him because the poor missionary was reputed to have an unsavory ecclesiastical reputation. Despite that very rudely expressed opinion, Bishop Carroll did not hesitate to request many favors from Father Gibault. Rebuffed by both Canada and Baltimore, Gibault successfully sought sacerdotal employment from the major ecclesiastical superior of Spanish Louisiana. By that late date, 1792, Gibault was a consummately experienced missionary with over two decades of frontier labor behind him. He found it most trying to be subject to his local Spanish superior at Ste. Geneviève, Father James Maxwell, a stickler for proper protocol and a hotheaded Irishman to boot. Gibault's last years, spent at New Madrid, were, consequently, one long series of petty annoyances.

Certainly, then, Pierre Gibault may be properly described as an historical enigma. Perhaps that inescapable fact explains why no historian has hitherto attempted a full-length biography of the man. Yet, Gibault is an important, if minor, character in the history of the War of Independence. As such, he deserves more than a passing footnote. Readers will not find in this book completely definitive answers to all the questions proposed regarding Pierre Gibault. Perhaps, however, they will come to know the man better.

## THE ILLINOIS COUNTRY

Writing to the minister of marine, comte de Maurepas, on July 25, 1733, Jean-Baptiste Le Moyne, sieur de Bienville, governor of the French colony of Louisiana, predicted: "I do not doubt that Illinois will in a short time become the most considerable settlement of the colony."[1] By the term *Illinois*, Bienville wished to designate the area of the Mississippi Valley between the Alleghenies and the Rocky Mountains and from about the mouth of the Missouri River to the confluence of the Ohio and the Mississippi.[2] Well might Bienville expect the Country of the Illinois, as the colonial French called it, to become in time the residence of thousands of French subjects. The roughly 200,000 square miles of the area, which the French could be said to have effectively occupied before 1763, has hardly an agricultural rival anywhere in the world.[3] The temperate climate, the vast, fertile, open prairies, the deep, rich soil, the numerous streams and navigable rivers made the territory a veritable paradise in an era when agriculture was the world's basic economic resource.

Centuries before Louis Jolliet and Father Jacques Marquette paddled down the mighty Mississippi aboriginal folk occupied the Illinois Country as the massive Monks Mound near Cahokia, Illinois, and effigy mounds scattered through Wisconsin, Illinois, Indiana, and Ohio amply demonstrate.[4] These ancient peoples enjoyed a level of culture much higher than that of the Algonkin tribes which came into possession of the area long before Europeans discovered the country. The Algonkin were, however, apparently greatly influenced by their predecessors for the aborigines found in the Illinois Country in the last quarter of the seventeenth century were reputed to be culturally superior to those contacted by the French in the St. Lawrence Basin.[5] The Kaskaskia, Cahokia, Tamaroa, Michigamea, and their Miami relatives were a sedentary folk dwelling in villages, cultivating corn, beans, melons, and squash.[6] Their need for meat and hides for clothing was supplied by the abundant game present. Perhaps because they came by their livelihood rather easily, they were not accustomed to travel widely by land nor did they commonly use the rivers as arteries of communication. Hence, though northern Algonkin were highly skilled in the construction and employment of birchbark canoes, these Indians normally made only balky pirogues of hollowed logs. Their code of ethics was somewhat more refined than that of aboriginal bands to the north. In common with most North American aboriginal tribes, they firmly believed in their dreams and in the fact that each one of them possessed a personal diety who protected them for the whole of their lives. Polygamy was commonly practiced, but promiscuity of women was severely punished. Father Claude Allouez, the first Jesuit missionary to learn of these Indians, delightedly reported: "Of all the spirits to whom they offer sacrifice, they honor with a very special worship one who is preeminent above all others, as they maintain, because he is the maker of all things."[7] That quite incorrect analysis of the religious beliefs of the Indians of the Illinois Country, plus the factual discovery of copper in the Lake Superior region, as well as the missionary's report of a great river in that country, were impelling reasons why the French began to explore the area south of Sault Ste. Marie.

From 1673 forward French interest in the Illinois Country developed with increasing intensity. That year, Louis Jolliet, accompanied by Father Jacques Marquette and five laymen, located the Mississippi River, mapped its major length and, on the return journey, traversed the entire length of the Illinois River. On that river, opposite Starved Rock, near the present Utica, Illinois, the explorers met the Kaskaskia who so impressed Marquette that he promised to return and establish a mission among them.[8] However, neither of these two pathfinders participated in the expansion of New France southward into the Illinois Country. Fulfilling his promise, Marquette returned to the Kaskaskia at Easter, 1675, but he was already so ill that he stayed only five days before starting northward. Death overtook him at Ludington, Michigan, on Saturday, May 18, 1675. Louis Jolliet, returning to Quebec in the summer of 1674, sought strenuously for land concessions and trading privileges in the vast area he had added to the French crown at his own expense. The prize went, however, to a favorite of Governor Frontenac, Robert Cavelier, sieur de La Salle.

Whatever his hostile contemporaries thought or unsympathetic historians have written concerning him, La Salle was the father of the Illinois Country. Beginning in 1678, when the crown authorized him to pursue the discovery of the western and southern reaches of New France, at his own expense, until 1683,

8

when La Salle left the area, his efforts were responsible for opening the country to the French. During his years in the area La Salle erected several forts, each at a geographically strategic position, which later developed into permanent French settlements.[9] Within the boundaries of his seigniory, whose capital was Fort St. Louis, he issued land grants to several of his companions. Though they did little or nothing toward establishing permanent residences, some intermarried with local dusky maidens and accustomed the Indians to the presence of the French with whom they established enduring trade relations. The trading aspect of La Salle's venture, however financially unsuccessful for him, served an important function for the future of the area. Because the Indians there could procure trade goods from them, the aborigines developed a loyalty to the French which endured. Consequently, with few exceptions, missionaries and settlers alike suffered very little from their Indian neighbors throughout the eighteenth century.

Though the Indians of the Illinois Country were generally friendly toward the French who invaded their country, evangelizing them advanced very slowly. After Marquette's fleeting visit to the Kaskaskia in 1675 no missionary contacted them until the great Father Claude Allouez arrived for a brief stay in 1677.[10] Returning in 1678, Allouez appears to have remained two consecutive years.[11] The true protoapostle of the Illinois Country, however, was Father Jacques Gravier, the Jesuit missionary who was sent, in 1687, to evangelize the aborigines of the Illinois Country and remained there until 1705, except for three years, 1695 to 1698, spent at St. Ignace mission as the superior of the whole Ottawa mission.[12] When Fort St. Louis was abandoned, Gravier relocated his mission near the newly established fort erected quite near the present Peoria, Illinois, where the Indians removed their village to within the shadow of the new fort.[13] There he was joined, in 1696, by Father Julien Binneteau whose excessive missionary labors caused his demise on December 24,

1699.[14] A fellow Jesuit, Pierre Pinet, also came to the Illinois Country in 1696, establishing the mission of the Guardian Angels at the mouth of the Chicago River so that the Wea, Miami, and other aboriginal bands frequenting the area might the more easily be evangelized. For reasons yet undiscovered, Governor Frontenac ordered that mission to be promptly abandoned. When Father Gravier protested to Bishop Laval, Frontenac withdrew his order, but the mission was permanently abandoned in 1700.[15] During that same year the Kaskaskia migrated southward settling some distance inland above the confluence of the Kaskaskia River and the Mississippi.[16] At its new and final location the mission of the Immaculate Conception was maintained by the Jesuits for the next sixty-three years during which Frenchmen settled near it, firmly establishing a village of their own.

During 1699, a year before the removal of the Jesuit mission to Kaskaskia, a new missionary group entered the Mississippi Valley from Quebec. These priests, to whom Bishop Laval confided the administration of the diocesan seminary, were members of a religious congregation known as the Sociéte des Missions-Etrangères. Since caring for French-Canadian candidates for the priesthood offered only indirect mission work, the priests obtained permission from Bishop Jean-Baptiste Saint-Vallier, Laval's successor, to establish missions in the Mississippi Valley where the Jesuits were already laboring.[17] On December 8, 1699, Father François de Montigny and his two companion priests, Antoine Davion and Jean François Busson de St. Côsme, founded the mission of the Holy Family among the Tamaroa near the location of Cahokia, Illinois. From that day to this there has been a Catholic church dedicated to the Holy Family at that site.[18] These dedicated missionaries extended their apostolate to include aborigines of the Missouri River and southward from Cahokia toward New Orleans. The Jesuits, who had been originally charged with exclusive responsibility for evangelizing the Indians in the Mississippi Valley, protested the presence of the new group until 1701 when a committee of French bishops decided that the two groups should work together harmoniously.[19] The mission of the Holy Family prospered, not so significantly as an Indian center but as a gathering place for French-Canadians who, after 1700, began to settle in the Mississippi Valley in some numbers.

While La Salle and his chief lieutenant, Henry Tonty, controlled the Illinois Country, no effort was made to give the few French settled there any sort of civil government. The first step toward direct royal jurisdiction was taken in 1712 when Philippe de Rigault, marquis de Vaudreuil, governor of New France, sent the sieur de Liette with a small military force to establish a permanent fort in the Illinois Country as a means of preventing British traders, as well as French renegades, from weaning the Indians away from the French.[20] Between 1712 and 1717, when Antoine Crozat's monopoly of Louisiana existed, Antoine de la Mothe Cadillac, governor of that colony, exercised some tenuous control of the Illinois Country, spending eight months visiting there in 1715.[21] In 1718, after the self-styled financial wizard, John Law, acquired monopolistic control of the area, the Illinois Country was formally incorporated into the colony of Louisiana. Though Law's financial house of cards collapsed by 1720, the Louisiana colony, including the Illinois Country, finally received organized civil-military control under the competent direction of Jean-Baptiste Le Moyne, sieur de Bienville, newly appointed governor of Louisiana.

Between 1718 and 1722, the internal government of the colony of Louisiana evolved through a series of stages until quite permanent institutions emerged. The major military and civil executive of the colony was the royally appointed governor, charged with general direction of the colony as well as responsibility for all relations with the Indians. Assisting, but somewhat independent, was the *commissaire-ordonnateur*, a counterpart of the intendant of New France. This official exercised jurisdiction over finances, public order, and judicial action. Associated with these were a military engineer in chief, responsible for defense, a first counsel, in charge of internal commerce, a counsel for import and export, a third, responsible for the colonists, also a fourth, charged with ordering religious matters, a fifth, caring for civil justice, and a sixth who functioned as a referee between disputants. These, plus the requisite clerks, notaries, and the like, constituted the colony's Superior Council. This body functioned as a French parlement for the registry of royal decrees as well as a final court of appeal within the colony.[22] The guiding legal principal in the colony derived from the *coutume de Paris*, originally the common law in force in the city of Paris and its dependencies.[23] The application of that particular *coutume*, or code of law, was most fortunate for of the more than 200 such *coutumes* then recognized in various areas of France that of Paris conferred more rights on the subjects than any other.[24]

For the administration of the French settlements and the Indians outside of the capital, New Orleans, the colony of Louisiana was divided into nine districts which, in turn, were gathered into four general military commanderies. In each district the military commandant exercised the major authority, assisted by a judge, a royal notary, a *commis* or clerk in charge of trade and commerce, and a *garde-magasin* or storekeeper. The latter managed the local royal warehouse from which the villagers procured products unavailable locally. Indians, too, traded there or, possibly, received from its stock presents granted them in the name of the king of France. Since little actual money circulated in the whole colony, purchases were normally made by exchange in kind at price levels set at Paris or New Orleans.[25]

The above proliferation of officialdom would lead to the conclusion that French colonial administration, even in the Illinois Country, was securely centralized. In fact, however, in those areas of human life which intimately affected the villag-

ers, the residents exercised a surprising amount of local demo-
cratic autonomy. In that distant corner of the French world no
landed gentry exercised ancient feudal rights over the peas-
antry, imposing taxes or handing down arbitrary justice. From
necessity much local government came into the hands of the people themselves. Since 1659, when the French crown declared all
villages to be minors under the guardianship of the king, each
village democratically elected a syndic or village spokesman
who represented his village in lawsuits. Because there was little
reason for such adjudications in the Illinois Country, the office
of syndic evolved into a sort of local mayor elected by the vote
of every male over fourteen. Any business pertaining to the
whole community was discussed at an open meeting presided
over by the syndic. Such matters as when to begin plowing,
planting, and harvesting, when and how to repair roads, and the
like, were determined. Decisions of the meeting were recorded
by the royal notary and the syndic was held responsible for seeing to the execution of the matters. For handling all ecclesiastical affairs the people elected *marguilliers* or church wardens
who were responsible for the physical care of the church and all
expenses incurred in its upkeep. Thus, in actual practice the
French residing in the Illinois Country had about as much experience in managing their own civil affairs as the New England
villagers, except that in New England the franchise was much
more restricted than was the case in the Mississippi Valley. That
factor may well explain why the French habitants readily accepted the institutions introduced to them when the area became
a part of the nascent United States.

Whence came the French who settled in the Mississippi
Valley; how many were there in, say, the mid-eighteenth century; how did they support themselves; and what sort of life did
they lead? As early as 1674 at least a few coureurs de bois, un-
licensed fur traders from Quebec or Montreal, were already in
the area.[26] On his various expeditions to the Illinois Country,

La Salle brought with him quite a large number of men.[27] Some of these were killed by Indians, but others deserted and were apparently never heard of again. When La Salle left the Mississippi Valley, his loyal lieutenant, Tonty, strove to continue the line of forts built by his commander. That, of course, required continual recruitment of men. Some few laymen were brought into the area by Jesuit missionaries as well as by the priests in charge of the mission at Cahokia. Though certainly some of these shadowy immigrants made the Illinois Country their home, none can be said to have done so of set purpose.

Soon after the opening of the eighteenth century settlers began to arrive in some numbers. In December 1718, for example, Pierre Duqué, sieur de Boisbriant, newly appointed commandant of the Illinois Country, reached Kaskaskia, accompanied by a hundred soldiers plus government officials, engineers, and craftsmen.[28] He it was who erected the first Fort Chartres situated some fifteen miles north of the Jesuit mission of the Immaculate Conception at Kaskaskia. Naturally a small village immediately sprang up in the vicinity of the fort. In 1721, Boisbriant procured a tract of land, about a league square, located a dozen miles north of the new fort. This he gave to his nephew, Jean Sainte Thérèse Langois, who founded there the village of Prairie du Rocher not long before 1734. In 1723, Philippe François Renault, a wealthy Parisian banker, planning to exploit the supposed mineral wealth of the Illinois Country, reached Kaskaskia, accompanied by 200 laborers and a contingent of Negro slaves purchased at Santo Domingo.[29] On one of his two grants of land, that nearer Fort Chartres, he set up the village of St. Philippe which became his headquarters.[30] On his other grant, on the west bank of the Mississippi, he began a lead mining operation around which developed the village of Ste. Genevieve.[31] At about the same time the governor of Louisiana, Périer, induced François Margane de la Valtrie, sieur de Vincennes, to erect a fort on the lower Wabash River as a means of

14

preventing the English from controlling that area.[32] There, too, Frenchmen settled and developed a village.

The population of these several villages grew very slowly. A census taken in 1723 showed a population of only 334 men, women, and children living in all the French settlements taken together. By 1732 that figure was increased to about 600.[33] A very careful census taken in 1746 showed that in the Illinois Country there were 749 men, women, and children of French extraction, 440 Negro slaves, and 157 Indians living in bondage.[34] When the British came into possession of the Illinois Country, a census was taken in 1767 which seems to indicate that the population numbered upwards of 2,000.[35]

As the population of the area increased sources of livelihood for the inhabitants necessarily modified. At first the only source of income was trading with the aborigines. But that quite rapidly declined because the country did not nurture the proper sort of fur-bearing animals in quantity. Besides, what peltries were gathered proved to be of an inferior quality. La Salle and others expected to reap rich profits from cloth spun from buffalo shearings. The Indians made a rough cloth from buffalo wool, but the coarse hair did not lend itself to commercial processing in Europe. By force of circumstances, therefore, as well as by royal encouragement, people in the Illinois Country turned to farming and stock raising as their chief occupation. By 1732 there was a well-established trade between the area and New Orleans whereby farmers shipped milled grains, salted beef and pork, tallow, and bear oil to the capital. There the products were exchanged for yard goods, tools, powder and shot, dishes, harnesses, and even some household furniture.[36]

In their several villages farmers continued the arrangement of their fields and dwellings which they knew in Canada. Fields were laid out in long narrow strips, each fronting on a' river or stream wherever possible. For mutual protection, the farmers dwelt together in villages rather than in isolated cabins on their individual lands. Dwellings were clustered around the church before which was the village common. Nearby was a common field where all domestic animals grazed under the care of young children or perhaps an ancient Negro or Indian slave. Considering the quite primitive farming equipment available, wooden plows sparingly shod with iron, for example, it is surprising that in a good year the Illinois Country farmers shipped as much as 200,000 pounds of flour to New Orleans.[37]

Not everyone supported himself exclusively by farming. In the more populous villages, such as Kaskaskia and Cahokia, some gained at least a part of their incomes as craftsmen. At Kaskaskia, for example, after 1724, there were found gunsmiths, carpenters, masons, blacksmiths, locksmiths, master joiners, roofers, sawyers, millers, barber surgeons, tailors, tavern keepers, and at least one wigmaker.[38] Also, the villages were frequently visited by the floating population of voyageurs, Indian traders, and crews of the river freighters, either canoes, bateaux, or rafts which carried local produce to New Orleans and brought back the goods ordered there by the villagers. As could be expected, that restless breed frequently disturbed the pastoral calm by their roistering. On the whole, the village folk probably welcomed the transients who spent their wages freely.

Though life in the French villages of the Illinois Country may have been a far cry from the Arcadian idyll some historians seem to portray it, one can quite safely think of it as reasonably pleasant. Social relations must have been very comfortable since there was almost a complete absence of class distinctions. The only group even faintly approaching a gentry was the commandant, his lady, and perhaps a selected few subordinates. Holidays, almost always ecclesiastical feasts, were celebrated with games and evening dances which even the pastor was expected to attend, at least briefly. New Year's Day, Mardi Gras, and every wedding occasioned great merriment. These French loved to drink wine and play cards, gambling for large stakes. There seems to have been little violent crime though lawsuits were frequent. Nonetheless, the Illinois Country was a true frontier where danger always lurked, if not from Indians, certainly from hardship, illness, serious accidents, and sudden, violent death. Women aged quickly and only the hardy child survived. This rugged French population manifested all the vices common to every frontier, but there was a significant difference. Religion permeated their lives. A man might disobey God's commandments, but he admitted frankly that his conduct was wrong. He might not be faithful to his wife, but he also did not excuse his infidelity. All in all, the French in the Illinois Country were a rugged, hardy, independent lot.

III

---

IF THERE BE NO PRIEST,

WHO WILL AVERT THE WRATH

OF A JUST GOD?

During the night of September 23, 1763, a courier from New Orleans reached Fort Chartres, the seat of government for the Illinois District of the French colony of Louisiana, carrying orders from Nicolas Chauvin de la Frénière,[1] colonial attorney general, ordering Etienne Pierre Marafret Laissard,[2] local substitute attorney, to put into effect the orders of a decree promulgated by the colony's Superior Council, on July 9, 1763, expelling, immediately, all Jesuits. The following morning, at "... eight or nine o'clock ... [Laissard] ... read to ... the superior [of the Illinois mission, Father Philippe Watrin] ... the decree of condemnation ... he made him [Watrin] at once leave the room to put the seal upon it; the same thing was done with the other missionaries who happened to be in the house."[3] The decree, among other charges, accused the missionaries of belonging to ". . . an Institute declared incompatible with the principles of all well-ordered states, perilous to the safety of our kings, and pretending to be independent of all tribunals."[4] The Jesuit missionaries had, according to the decree:

> Everywhere in America . . . earned the reproach that their missions had been designed less for the conversion of the natives than for the increase of power of their Order. . . . they have made very few conversions in the posts of this colony, where their ambition has often been the cause of dissensions. . . .
>
> These facts, and above all their injurious monopoly of authority . . . would suffice . . . to proscribe forever from this colony, men who live under an Institute, the rules of which are contrary to good order, outrageous to royal authority, perilous for the safety of our kings, and independent of all tribunals. . . .[5]

For these heinous crimes, proven against the Jesuits to the satisfaction of all but one member of the colony's Superior Council,[6] the king's attorney general demanded that:

> . . . the *soi-disants* Jesuits [be commanded] under penalty of constraint as disturbers of the public peace, . . . be shipped away by the first vessel bound for France . . . that description and enumeration of the real and movable property [of the Jesuits] . . . be made . . . and sold and that the proceeds of the sale . . . be given to the king to be used and disposed of as it shall please the king our master, without prejudice to the legitimate claims of . . . creditors. . . .[7]

Enforcing the decree banishing them from Louisiana came as no great surprise to the Jesuit missionaries. This was but another in a long series of attacks by churchmen and European governments. Since its foundation in 1540, the unprecedented expansion of the Society of Jesus, both in membership and in the striking success of its multifarious endeavors, engendered at least a modicum of envy in some members of older orders within the Church. Theological discussions, begun during the late sixteenth and accelerated during the following century, found competent Jesuit theologians opposing others, equally competent, who, with some justification, began to hold that Jesuits assumed a corporate position which each member defended with unswerving loyalty. Consequently, it came to be believed that Jesuits considered themselves an ecclesiastical elite, individually humble enough, but as a group overweaningly proud. However justified this sort of petty jealousy was, it objectively existed, particularly, perhaps, because Jesuits actually were quite influential. In their many colleges they educated great numbers of the nobility as well as the sons of the increasingly influential bourgeois class.

The ideal educational product sought by the Jesuits was the thoroughly cultured, High Renaissance gentleman, eloquent, intellectually keen, completely dedicated to the principles of Christianity. Because the system filled a crying need and proved far superior to any other available, Jesuit colleges in large numbers were established on the continent of Europe.[8] By the mid-eighteenth century there were 621 throughout the world, 89 of them in France. To staff the faculties of these, the Society of Jesus imparted to its members excellent intellectual and spiritual training. As a result, many Jesuits became noted scholars in various fields of learning, including the exact sciences.[9] Perhaps due to the social status of most of their students, the Jesuits themselves did not clearly perceive the growing social unrest in Europe. Jesuit faculties neither modified their curricula to meet changing conditions nor did they effectively refute the principles motivating the philosophy of the Enlightenment as that movement developed. Thus, during the eighteenth century, the great edifice of Jesuit education became a sort of first-line defense for the crumbling Ancien Régime and an annoying stumbling block to the advanced thinkers of the new Age of Enlightenment.

20

Whatever advancement the Enlightenment might have subsequently produced by stimulating intellectual interest in fields other than philosophy and theology, in essence the movement's early champions were either agnostics or crusading opponents of structured Christianity as they knew it. Their major target was, of course, the Catholic Church, which, to paraphrase, was the "infamous thing" which must be crushed. Athwart the Enlightenment juggernaut were Jesuit writers, preachers, and teachers, for over a century the most articulate defenders of orthodoxy and spiritual supremacy of the papacy. So long as the conflict was confined to a battle of books and pamphlets, the existence of the Society of Jesus was not threatened. But when major governmental officials became devotees of the Enlightenment they promptly perceived that the principles proposed by the new philosophy furnished an effective weapon with which to drastically reduce or completely eliminate the influence of the Church on governments. Opposing the politicians were the Jesuits who could employ their writers, their colleges, and their countless loyal alumni to mount an effective counterattack.

Attacks against the Jesuits by royal ministers of various governments in Europe did not appear in the form of treatises demonstrating the unreasonableness of moral absolutes. Rather, there was launched a campaign of insinuation. It was inferred that Jesuit confessors of crowned heads were, in reality, undercover agents of a vast, secret conspiracy plotting to gain political control of all Europe. Undoubtedly some Jesuits placed in these delicate positions did allow pietistic queen-regents and weak-willed princes to involve them unduly in purely state matters. Also, there was the inevitable handful of imprudent Jesuits, the bane of every such organization, who gained nothing personally by their positions, but gave flesh to the purely imaginative, wily Jesuit who insidiously manipulated international affairs. Aided by such propaganda, European governments, one by one, expelled the Jesuits from their countries and, finally, on July 21,

21

1773, procured from the pope, Clement XIV, the brief *Dominus ac redemptor* whereby the Society of Jesus was suppressed throughout the world.[10]

In France the Jesuits had never enjoyed the complete support of the crown, despite the fact that, for a century and more, traditionally a Jesuit was the king's confessor. Major governmental officials were normally cold in their attitude toward the Society of Jesus because the organization unwaveringly supported the papacy against any attempt of the French to reduce Catholicity in the country to a national church independent of Rome.[11] Besides, during the seventeenth century the Jesuits had incurred the bitter enmity of the Jansenists whose remnants, during the eighteenth century, joined forces with the devotees of the Enlightenment. In their view the Jesuits in France constituted an annoying, powerful obstacle to any ideological advancement. For these dedicated disciples of the Enlightenment, merely discrediting the intellectual position of the Jesuits was not enough; only the expulsion of all members of the Society of Jesus from France would satisfy them. Much as this element in France desired the expulsion of the Jesuits, the deed must be done on legal grounds by means of decisions won from the courts before judges. And they were enabled to accomplish their objective because of the incredible imprudence of a Jesuit missionary in the Antilles, Père Antoine La Valette.

Born in 1707, Antoine La Valette, who became a Jesuit at eighteen, was sent to the mission on the island of Martinique, in 1741, just 101 years after the Jesuits began their apostolic labors on that Caribbean possession of France. Besides caring for the spiritual welfare of the French *colons*, the missionaries sought to convert the thousands of Negro slaves imported by the planters whose major exports were sugar and coffee. Over the decades the Jesuits also acquired plantations which were tilled by slaves and whose produce supported the Martinique mission centers. There was nothing unusual or even uncanonical about

22

this practice which was commonly employed by missionaries, whether Jesuits, Franciscans, or others, in various areas of the world far distant from Europe.[12] However, both canon law and the decrees of the Society of Jesus strictly forbade engaging in such enterprises solely for profit, to say nothing of unabashed speculation. And therein lay La Valette's downfall.

In 1746, five years after his arrival, La Valette was appointed procurator or treasurer of the mission at Martinique. He apparently decided that the mission's finances were in such desperate straits that the only possible solution was improving the output of the Jesuit plantations. He succeeded so well that French planters registered complaints, accusing La Valette of engaging in business in a manner contrary to canon law. In 1753, the year La Valette was appointed superior of the Jesuits on the island of Martinique, he was summoned to Europe, not only by the Jesuit general, Ignatius Visconti, but also by the French minister of marine, Antoine Louis Rouillé, to answer the charges. Having successfully defended himself, La Valette returned to the island, in 1755, where he found that the financial situation had gone from bad to worse. Wherefore he began to speculate on a large scale, borrowing great sums from banking houses, chiefly at Marseilles. With his borrowed capital La Valette purchased more lands and more slaves, confidently expecting to meet his obligations out of the produce. His scheme failed miserably when an epidemic wiped out great numbers of his field hands and the Seven Years' War gave British privateers opportunity to prey on French shipping. Several vessels carrying mission produce were captured with disastrous results to La Valette's precarious juggling act. Finally, in 1760, the whole house of cards collapsed. When several of La Valette's creditors sued, the French lower courts decreed that the whole Society of Jesus in France was obliged to assume La Valette's debts.

At that juncture the provincial of the Jesuit province of France committed a tactical blunder. According to ecclesiastical

law, which the French crown recognized, each Jesuit house was an independent legal entity responsible for its own financial responsibilities, but not for any other.[13] Legally, therefore, the mission of Martinique was solely responsible for the financial disaster La Valette's imprudence caused. Initially the Jesuit mission treasurer at Paris proposed to pay the debts incurred, but, when it was ascertained that the sum amounted to nearly $1,000,000, the provincial at Paris, of which the Martinique mission was a dependency, determined to appeal the decision of lower courts to the Parlement of Paris. That was a fatal mistake for many of the jurists sitting on the court were bitter enemies of the Jesuits. In a series of decisions handed down between May 5 and August 19, 1761, the Parlement decreed that not only was the whole Society of Jesus in France liable for La Valette's debts but, further, French subjects might not, henceforth, join the Jesuits and that the educational institutions under their charge must be closed. On August 6, 1762, the Parlement of Paris issued a decree ordering the extinction of the Society in France and confiscating its property.

Though the French government must have expected that revenues from confiscated Jesuit property would not only reimburse La Valette's creditors but would also help pay some of the expenses incurred by France in pursuit of the Seven Years' War, such was far from the case. Often enough large buildings housing Jesuit colleges simply had no purchasers. Frequently, endowments supporting the colleges were so entailed by legal technicalities that sequestering the funds would incur lengthy litigation. Much Jesuit property, such as scientific instruments, libraries, and the like, while valuable in themselves, were not easily converted into ready cash. Also, to avoid the charge of heartlessness, the government granted each of the 4,000 French Jesuits an average daily stipend of 20 sous.[14] When La Valette's creditors perceived that they were not likely to be reimbursed from revenues at home they had recourse to the king, petition-

ing that Jesuit properties in the French colonies be preempted for their benefit.[15] Wherefore, in June 1763, Louis XV issued *lettres-patents* declaring Jesuit properties in Martinique, Guadeloupe, Louisiana, Cayenne, and elsewhere forfeit to the crown and ordered his Superior Council in each colony to implement his directive.[16]

Many months before that royal decree was registered the French government had determined to seize all property possessed by the Jesuits in the colonies. Despite the fact that Louisiana had been ceded to Spain on November 3, 1762, early in 1763 France sent to that colony a new director general, Jean Jacques Blaise Dabbadie, and a new attorney general, Frénière, both of whom were instructed before sailing from France to seize all Jesuit property in the colony of Louisiana.[17] That sequestration would not realize a very large sum since the Jesuits in the colony owned only two parcels of land, one at New Orleans and the other situated a short distance from Fort Chartres in the Illinois Country.[18] At New Orleans, the sale of the Jesuit holdings, including land, domestic animals, slaves, and every stick of furniture, netted 955,752 livres calculated in the colony's inflated money. At Fort Chartres the auction of the Jesuit property and effects brought about 40,000 livres. As could have been easily predicted, by the time local debts were paid and expenses of the sales were deducted very little of the money was forwarded to the crown.

Having deprived the Jesuits in the colony of their apostolate and their homes, nothing remained for the officials to accomplish except expelling them. Before December 1763, the Jesuits stationed at New Orleans obliged by sailing to France, with the exception of the superior, Baudouin.[19] A native Canadian, he had no wish to go to France where he had neither friends nor relatives. Since he could not be returned to Canada which had become a British possession, the aged and infirm missionary was allowed to remain at New Orleans for his few

remaining years. The Jesuits in the Illinois Country, except Aubert, were shipped off to New Orleans on November 24, arriving there on December 21. Though treated kindly, especially by the Capuchins, the missionaries soon ". . . perceived that their departure was desired."[20] On February 6, 1764, all but Fathers La Morinie and Meurin took ship for France on the *Minerve* which reached San Sebastián on April 6. La Morinie, a poor sailor, was permitted to wait for spring when he too departed. Father Sebastien Meurin, however, begged earnestly to be allowed to return to his neophytes, willingly accepting any restrictive conditions the Superior Council might see fit to impose. ". . . he knew in what danger the Illinois neophytes were of soon forgetting religion if they remained long without missionaries."[21] Also, unless at least one missionary was allowed to remain there would be no priest anywhere in the vast area between Lake Superior and New Orleans.

Father Sebastien Meurin merits some brief biographical notice. Born at Charleville in Champagne on December 26, 1709, he probably received his early education at the Jesuit college in his hometown where Father Jacques Marquette had taught from 1661 to 1663. On September 28, 1726, three months before his seventeenth birthday, he entered the Jesuit novitiate at Nancy. Completing the novitiate in the fall of 1728, he spent the following eight years teaching for various periods of time in the Jesuit colleges at Nancy, Chaumont, Auxerre, Reims, and Verdun. From 1736 to 1740 he studied theology at Reims where, probably, he received sacerdotal ordination, quite likely in 1739. In the fall of 1741 Meurin sailed for New Orleans, arriving in November of that year.[22] After the customary year of apprenticeship, Meurin was sent to the Illinois Country where he spent the remainder of his life evangelizing the Indians and caring for the souls of the French residing there.

When the contingent of Jesuits was sent down to New Orleans from the Illinois Country in 1763, Father Meurin obedi-

ently accompanied them. But, arrived at the capital of the colony, he promptly began begging the civil officials to allow him to return to the field of his labors, willing to accept almost any conditions they might wish to impose so long as they let him go back. Revealing his motivation in a letter to Jean-Olivier Briand, bishop of Quebec, four years later, he explained: "Seeing that it [the Illinois Country] was going to be abandoned and be without a pastor, I solicited during one month and obtained, particularly on account of the savages, the right to return here."[23] The conditions posited by the Superior Council were almost impossible. Meurin was required to reside on the west bank of the wide Mississippi, at Ste. Genevieve, though the major population, both French and Indians, whom the missionary sacrificed so much to serve, lived up and down the east side of the river.[24] Further, Father Meurin was obliged to ". . . promise and sign that [he] should no longer recognize [any] other ecclesiastical superior than the reverend superior of the Capuchins who alone had and would have all jurisdiction [in the colony of Louisiana]. . . ."[25] The first directive, regarding his place of residence presented a problem of inconvenience. Even though Meurin was not quite fifty-four, he was already aged by his labors and chronically unwell. Yet he bore the added burden uncomplainingly. But the question of ecclesiastical jurisdiction could not be dismissed lightly since on it hinged the sacramental validity of his priestly functions. Obliged to accept the word of the Superior Council, Meurin agreed to submit to the ecclesiastical jurisdiction of the Capuchin superior, provided he would eventually be forwarded documentary evidence proving the authenticity of that official's asserted position.[26] "It is," wrote Meurin later, "on this condition that I signed, adding that when it should please his holiness to give the jurisdiction to the highest chief of the Negroes I should be submissive to him as to one meriting more than bishops; . . ."[27] Troubled in spirit, Father Meurin left New Orleans in mid-February 1764 and dutifully took up residence at Ste. Genevieve whence he sought to bring religious comfort to the whole central Mississippi Valley.[28]

For the following three years Sebastien Meurin ministered to the parish of Ste. Genevieve, but each spring and fall he visited all the French villages on the banks of the Mississippi, including the settlement at St. Louis, founded in 1764. Often enough at other times, however, he was summoned to one or other village to comfort the dying.[29] Expending himself thus was none too pleasing to the parishioners at Ste. Genevieve who alone contributed to Meurin's support.[30] Nor were his taxing efforts for the spiritual welfare of other villages greatly appreciated. A faction at Kaskaskia ". . . refused to recognize him as pastor, saying he has no right to give them advice and that they are not obliged to listen to him."[31] On August 7, 1767, Jean-Olivier Briand, bishop of Quebec, in whose diocese the Illinois Country really belonged, wrote the Kaskaskians a sharply critical letter, threatening that unless they showed proper respect to their pastor, Father Meurin, the bishop would henceforth look upon them as ". . . members of my diocese who do not merit my attention; . . ."[32]

After three years of unremitting effort, Father Meurin's infirmities so weighed upon him that he sought, from every possible source, both sacerdotal recruits for his vast apostolate as well as clarification of his difficulty regarding ecclesiastical jurisdiction. Apparently, before leaving New Orleans, in February 1764, he petitioned the Holy See for ecclesiastical authority in favor of the Illinois Country. On September 4, 1765, Clement XIII granted Father Meurin ". . . for his country of the Illinois extraordinary faculties such as had never been granted to any bishops, vicars-apostolic or missionaries in America."[33] Seemingly, Meurin never learned of the papal decision for he continued assiduously, until 1767, seeking to regularize his jurisdictional position from sources in North America. In the meantime, Meurin, according to his own declaration, used ". . .

the authority I received from M. Mercier which was continued by MM. Laurent and Forget, the latter of whom verbally left me, at his departure, all he had received."[34] On learning of Briand's succession to the see of Quebec in 1766, Father Meurin wrote to the bishop, pleading for help and asking that one of the priests sent might be appointed the bishop's vicar-general for the Illinois Country. Only a month after the date of Meurin's letter to him, Briand replied, appointing Meurin himself to the office of vicar-general and promising to send the weary missionary young cohorts as soon as possible.[35]

Bishop Briand's gracious gesture created as many problems for poor Father Meurin as it solved. During the diplomatic jockeying antecedent to the Peace of Paris of 1763, France surrendered whatever claim she pretended to have over territory west of the Mississippi to Spain. In due time officials of the new owner assumed authority at Ste. Genevieve. Philippe François de Rastel, chevalier de Rocheblave, an opportunist if there ever was one, appointed Spanish commandant at Ste. Genevieve, pompously took umbrage, in mid-1767, when it became known that Father Meurin had been appointed vicar-general of the bishop of Quebec. Rocheblave officiously announced: "I know no English Bishop here, and in a post where I command, I wish no ecclesiastical jurisdiction recognized except that of the archbishop of Santo Domingo."[36] For his supposedly vicious crime of contacting the bishop of Quebec, Meurin was declared a state criminal with orders issued for his prompt arrest. Late in October 1767 the persecuted missionary fled by night to the east bank of the Mississippi. There, for his own protection as well as to further his apostolic work, he took the oath of allegiance to the king of England.[37]

Father Meurin's missionary life was far from pleasant during the coming few years. His poor health, failing sight, and declining mental faculties prevented him from journeying regularly to the various communities which he longed to serve. Besides, people in Canada with economic interests in the Illinois Country sought his good offices in their regard. For example, the priests of the Missions-Etrangères importuned him to obtain the restoration of their property at Cahokia which one of their members, François Forget du Verger, had quite illegally sold when he fled the Illinois Country in 1763.[38] When the property was up for sale a second time, Meurin, at the original owners' request, informed the British commandant, Brigadier John Forbes, of the owners' valid claim, but in vain. He also carried on a lengthy and, apparently, quite heated controversy with one Jean Baptiste Beauvais seeking to induce the latter to restore to ecclesiastical use the furnishings taken from the demolished church of the Immaculate Conception which had been the chapel for the Indians at their mission near Kaskaskia. In this, too, he was signally unsuccessful.[39] One senses in his letters regarding this matter how deeply pained the old missionary was to see the mission altar and its vestment cases put to profane use.

Possibly Father Meurin's greatest source of sorrow was the fact that the French habitants treated him with such little respect and consideration. He wrote to Bishop Briand:

> During the four years that I have ministered to these English parishes [those on the east bank of the Mississippi] I have received no tithes therefrom. I have lived only on the charity of some . . . I have always exhorted them to pay the tithes to the vestry board for the support of the churches and the missionary when he comes. They (I mean the rich ones) have always claimed not to owe anything when there is no resident pastor. I beg you to decide the case; otherwise three missionaries would not be able to live decently, or would be compelled to leave some villages abandoned.[40]

Despite these difficulties, Meurin hoped for a brighter future, provided the bishop sent sufficient priests to minister to the unruly flock for whom he had sacrificed so much. In his letter, he remarked:

I shall soon be unable to do anything more; but threatened beforehand, as I am, with being cast out when others shall come, I wish all the more ardently for them. I have always had the poor on my side. Priests will be at least as charitable as they, and God will assist me through them; or if He prefers (which would be more advantageous for me) He will cause me to share his abandonment . . . [I shall be] happy if I can receive the consolations of Christians, dying with Jesus Christ in the hands of one of his ministers.[41]

Even as Father Meurin was writing his letter of June 11, 1768, to Bishop Briand, Father Pierre Gibault was en route to join the failing old apostolic warrior. Shortly, Sebastien Louis Meurin would retire to Prairie du Rocher to live out his days, gently cared for by the members of his parish. He died, unattended by a priest, on February 23, 1777. Sixty-five years later, in 1842, his remains were transferred to the cemetery on the grounds of the Jesuit novitiate at Florissant, Missouri.[42]

## PIERRE GIBAULT

Poitiers, perched on a promontory of rugged old Jurassic rock, stands sentry over a natural invasion route from the port of La Rochelle to Paris. Its history reaches back to the days of Julius Caesar when the Picts, whose tribal title evolved into the present name of the town, were allies of the Romans in their conquest of present-day France. Aryan Visigoths once held the place as the seat of a kingdom and Charles Martel, in 732, routed the Moors near Tours, only sixty miles to the north. During the Hundred Years' War, on September 19, 1356, Edward, the Black Prince, son of Edward III of England, delivered a stunning defeat to the French, capturing King John, his son, his brother-in-law, Charles IV, king of Bohemia, and the flower of French chivalry. The forces of the Black Prince so ravaged the country that even they went hungry. When France was torn by civil strife, during the last quarter of the sixteenth century, Poitiers bore its share of suffering from the religious zealots of each of the contesting forces. Such is the background from which the ancestors of Pierre Gibault had their origins.

The first Gibault to emigrate to New France was Gabriel, Father Gibault's great-grandfather, who was born in 1641 in the parish of Notre Dame de Lusinan in the diocese of Poitiers. Though no one knows in exactly what year Gabriel came to Canada, when he was twenty-six, in 1667, he married Suzanne Durand at Quebec on October 31. The bride was only fourteen for she was born in 1653 at St. Sauveur de Montevillier in the diocese of Rouen.[1] In 1681, fourteen years after his marriage, Gabriel is known to have been a landholder on the seigniory of Laveltrie, an area surrounding the present city of Laveltrie, Canada, on the north bank of the St. Lawrence, some thirty miles northeast of Montreal.[2] The youngest of Gabriel's nine children, twin boys, Pierre and Gabriel, were baptized on May 14, 1680, at Repentigay, a village roughly ten miles below Montreal on the way to Quebec. Very little can be discovered about Pierre, the twin who was Father Gibault's grandfather, except that he married Marie Joseph Brunet. This couple were the parents of a son, Pierre, who was Father Gibault's father. The only record concerning that Pierre seems to be the date of his marriage, on November 14, 1735, to Marie Joseph St. Jean at Sorel, a small village at the mouth of the Richelieu River. Pierre and his wife, Marie Joseph, frequently moved their place of residence, for each of their children was born at a different location. Pierre, the subject of this study, was baptized at Montreal on April 7, 1737. His sister, Marie Joseph, was baptized at Baie-du-Febvre on December 10, 1740. The next child, Marie Louise, was baptized at St. François-du-Lac on January 27, 1751. Marie Angelique, the youngest daughter, was baptized at Ste. Croix on July 15, 1752.[3] Father Gibault had one brother, Jacques, about whom nothing can be discovered except the fact that the priest left property to Jacques in his will.[4]

Of Father Gibault's childhood and youth practically nothing can be discovered. Some historians assume that he attended the Jesuit college at Quebec. If so, he would have been there sometime between 1749, when he was twelve, until approximately 1755, when he was eighteen. These were the age brackets of those enrolled at the college for its complete curriculum.[5] If Gibault did not attend the college, it would be a mistake to assume that he received only a sketchy early education, perhaps nothing more than the ability to read and write, from the pastor in one or other parish. Though Peter Kalm, in his *Travels in North America*, probably exaggerated in depicting every little Canadian village as having a primary school in 1749, it is quite true that many communities actually did have a school.[6] There is, however, some reason to believe that Gibault received a good classical education. After his death an inventory was made of his extensive library which included a goodly number of treatises in Latin. Facility in that language would indicate his having acquired the skill in his youth.[7]

One should recall that during Gibault's growing years New France was almost constantly at war. During King George's War, 1740-1748, French colonials carried on raids against Maine and New England villages or defended themselves against similar attacks by the British colonists and their Indian allies. From 1754 to 1760, hundreds of French regulars and native Canadians engaged in a conflict involving the very existence of New France as a part of the possessions of the French crown. Since Gibault was a grown man of twenty-three when Vaudreuil, the last governor of Canada appointed by the king of France, was obliged to surrender the colony to the British at Montreal, on September 8, 1760, it is quite possible that Gibault saw service in the army during that war. Yet all we know about the period of his early manhood is that in 1759 he made a journey by canoe between Detroit and Michilimackinac, but in which direction and why we do not know.[8]

Why Pierre Gibault went to the Illinois Country in his youth can be only conjectured. He might have been there as a soldier or, again, simply as a member of a trading expedition. If the latter, he could have gone there as early as his fourteenth year. It was not at all uncommon for youths of even more tender age to be included in such ventures so that they might learn the trade. It is to be noted, also, that in New France a boy of fourteen was considered old enough to bear arms in the defense of the country. In his *L'Eglise du Canada*, Auguste Gosselin declares that Gibault was taken to the Illinois Country by his parents when the boy was quite young and after a few years brought back to Canada.[9]

Some have portrayed the young Pierre Gibault as a typical roistering coureur de bois who "got religion" in his more mature years. This conclusion is based on several statements made by Gibault in letters to his bishop, such as: "What joy for me to repair the time so ill-spent in my youth by the opportunity God offers me of better employment."[10] In itself, the remark does not necessarily imply any youthful dissipation. It could just as well mean that Gibault regretted that he had not been more religiously fervent as he grew up. The statement can hardly be taken as a parallel of St. Augustine's "How late have I loved Thee," which, in the saint's case, was objectively true. Whatever the facts, Pierre Gibault's future, perhaps even his ambition from childhood, was that of an ordained apostle in the Illinois Country, a career he began at the age of thirty-one.

The British conquest of Canada was as disruptive of ecclesiastical regularity as it was of civil affairs. When Quebec was attacked in 1759, Bishop Henri-Marie de Pontbriand retired to Montreal where he died on June 8, 1760. It was not until 1766 that a successor, Jean-Olivier Briand, occupied the vacant see. In the meantime, the Jesuit college, where the seminarians had taken their classes since the very beginning of the seminary, was requisitioned by the British and never completely restored to its original purpose. When the new bishop took charge of his diocese, one of his earliest acts was the reopening of the seminary under the care of the priests of the Missions-Etrangères. Two of the first aspirants for the priesthood were Pierre Gibault and a companion named Mauvide who did not persevere.

From the inception of his brief seminary training of a little more than two years, Pierre Gibault appears to have been destined for mission work in the Illinois Country. The priests of the Missions-Etrangères, who quite properly felt it their obligation to supply a priest for their abandoned Tamaroa mission at Cahokia, bore the expenses of Gibault's education.[11] The truncated course in theology which the mature Gibault received was ". . . hardly enough for a young priest destined to go alone so far away and so exposed to such great dangers."[12] However, the dire need for a missionary to assist the aging Meurin in the Illinois Country plus the eloquent pleadings of the people of Kaskaskia, to say nothing of the pathetic petition of the citizens of Vincennes, induced Bishop Briand to hasten Gibault's preparation. The neophyte was ordained to the priesthood on March 19, 1768.[13] On that day Gibault was four months and five days beyond his thirtieth birthday, certainly no wide-eyed fledgling. For a few weeks the newly ordained priest assisted at the cathedral in Quebec. But in early June 1768 Gibault was ready to depart for the Illinois Country.

Apparently it was with no little trepidation that Bishop Briand sent Father Gibault off to his mission field in the Illinois Country. The bishop wrote Father Meurin, announcing Gibault's appointment and requesting the old missionary's paternal care for the new recruit. "He is a young priest," the bishop said, "and I beg you to watch over him and tell me, in our Lord, whether or not he deserves my confidence. I would be terribly crushed if he turned out badly. He has made all sorts of fine promises to me and I love him. But I am not undisturbed about him."[14]

On May 15, 1768, when Gibault was about to depart, Bishop Briand gave him a lengthy letter replete with paternal advice and practical suggestions. Gibault was urged, above all, to be gentle for:

> . . . people never become Christians through violence, but by persuasion. . . . All fervent missionaries have been men of prayer. . . . without prayer you will not persevere. You will soon become insipid salt . . . Avoid showing preference for anyone and have no favorite families. As much as possible, do not be served by persons of the opposite sex, unless they be of advanced age and of irreproachable morals. I would prefer that you had none of them at all . . . Where religious principles permit you to give way, do not remain inflexible. . . . Do not permit the missionaries to engage in commerce . . . Discourage the people from harboring a visionary hope of the return of the French. On the contrary, incline them to great docility toward the [British] commandant and an attachment to the [present] government. . . . Exhort the people to engage in agriculture. This will render them sedentary and put them to work. . . . Encourage youth to marry early. This is the means of hindering dissolute living. . . . May God keep you in his holy grace and direct your steps.[15]

Between the lines in all of this one cannot help sensing that his ecclesiastical superior harbored a lack of complete confidence in Pierre Gibault. Justified or not, that attitude on the part of his superiors was to plague the missionary throughout the rest of his life. Yet it is next to impossible to put one's finger on precisely why. Perhaps Father Gibault was a man afflicted with a difficult temperament, quick to anger. It may have been that he was known to have been endowed with a spirit of independence. The attitude of his superiors could not have been engendered by any lack of moral probity on Gibault's part for during his long missionary career of well over thirty years his moral conduct was above reproach. Yet, from the very first Gibault was constantly under a cloud.

On May 30, 1768, only a day or two previous to Gibault's departure from Quebec, Bishop Briand issued him a formal document appointing him vicar-general for ". . . the regions commonly called Illinois and Tamaroa . . . [and] . . . all further places in our diocese to which you may come. . . ."[16] Father Gibault was granted the widest possible ecclesiastical jurisdiction which he was not to exercise, however, ". . . except as dependent on . . . Father Meurin . . . , our vicar-general for all these aforesaid places and for all others adjacent—even for all the regions of Louisiana—which have been clearly known hitherto to belong to our diocese. . . ."[17] Armed with that impressive document, Gibault set out for Montreal and the long, weary journey to the Illinois Country, probably on the last day of May or the first of June. Whether he went up the St. Lawrence to Montreal by canoe or traveled the 180 miles by road is not known. It is interesting to note that if he went by land the journey required four days and the coach fare was twenty sous.[18]

Arrived at Montreal, Father Gibault applied to the military governor for permission to travel to the Illinois Country. On June 7, 1768, he was issued the following document:

> By the Hon. Guy Carleton, Lieutenant Governor and commander in chief of the Province of Quebec, Brigadier General commanding His Majesty's Forces in the Northern District:
> The commander in chief of His Majesty's Forces in North America having been pleased to approve of a priest from this Province repairing to the Illinois for the comfort and satisfaction of the King's Roman Catholic subjects in those parts, who it is hoped will entertain a due sense of the care [he] showeth for their interests.
> These are therefore to permit Rev. Pierre Gibault a missionary priest, who has taken the oath of allegiance to His Majesty, together with Marie Gibault his mother and Louise Gibault his

sister, to pass from hence to the Illinois by way of Michilimack-
inac in a canoe with the baggage to them belonging; without hin-
drance or molestation; in which all officers commanding at the
several Forts and Posts, within the Northern District are required,
as those without said district are desired to be aiding and assisting
to him, in forwarding him to his aforementioned destination. He,
as well as the people with him, behaving as becometh.

Given under our hand and seal at Montreal this 7th Day of
June 1768.

> By the Brig. Gen'ls command.
> Guy Carleton
> H. T. Cramaché[19]

Gibault apparently spent most of the month of June 1768
at Montreal, collecting supplies for his mission. Since his
mother and his sister, Marie Louise, resided there, he undoubtedly visited them frequently. The missionary seems to have importuned his mother to accompany him, but that lady ". . . said
to me when I went to see her that her age, and even more her
will, were against her leaving her country."[20] But six days before Gibault was to depart from Montreal the mother came to
her son saying, ". . . that she would go to the other end of the
world with me rather than stay in her old age at the mercy of
this one and that one."[21] So Madam Gibault, by then a widow,
and her seventeen-year-old daughter, Marie Louise, packed
their effects and set out with Father Gibault for his mission in
the Illinois Country.

On approximately July 1, 1768, Pierre Gibault left Montreal in the company of an Illinois trader named Despains who
had promised the people of Kaskaskia that he would transport a
missionary to them at no cost to the priest provided the Kaskaskians reimbursed him.[22] The flotilla of canoes in which Gibault
traveled spent twenty-two miserable days beating up the St.
Lawrence, across Lake Ontario to Detroit, and thence up Lake
Huron to the present Mackinac City, Michigan.[23] Arriving there
on about July 21, the new priest had his first missionary experi-

39

ence which he described to Bishop Briand in a letter dated July 28, 1768:

Monseigneur:

I have the honor, at the moment of leaving this post, to assure Your Grace of my respects and to give you an account, as clearly as I can considering the inconvenience in which I find myself, of what I have accomplished here. Up to the present our journey has been very slow and laborious because of the quantity of rain we had from Montreal to Michilimackinac. We had twenty-two days of rain to say nothing of wind. The consoling thing is that we lacked nothing. That is, we had provisions [enough] to supply us without skimping whereas the canoemen who came before and after us were reduced to subsisting on *tripe de roche*.[24] On arriving at this post, after dining with the commander, I went to the confessional which I did not leave for ten hours and this is the only day I have left it that early.[25] I also had some baptisms to perform but only one marriage ceremony. I have had some distress and sorrow in my short sojourn here, but also some consolation. My distress arose from being unable to remain long enough to respond to the eagerness of the great number of *voyageurs* who asked me to hear their confessions. Some have not been to confession for from three to ten years. They have made every possible offer to retain me, promising to pay [the wages of] my people as far as the Illinois and offering to accompany me [there themselves] with two canoes. But, having orders from Your Grace for the Illinois only, I feared some trouble might arise through my fault. Four canoes of *voyageurs* should leave tomorrow morning with us which will go a hundred leagues from here. They have delayed a week expressly to go to confession. In a word, God has not been wholly forgotten by these people. All that is necessary is laborers, resolute to endure hunger and thirst and to keep perpetual Lent. I have not thus far left M. Despains and, as he would be much grieved if he could not arrive with me in the Illinois, I could remain here only a week. According to the news which I have received, my Lord, I expect to be well received. The Spanish have driven Father Meurin from their villages. The English commandant has received him graciously, except for that they would have sent him to the sea in less than twenty-four hours. As for me, I am delighted that he is [now] on my side [of the river]. I have been visited here by the savages of Father DuJonais [Du Jaunay]; they regret his loss as if it was the first day.[26] Those who speak French have come to confession; others wished to, but we could not understand each other. With all my heart I desire to reach my destination, to fulfill the wishes of God and those of Your Grace to whom I am with all respect and submission,

Your very humble and very obedient servant,
Gibault, priest.[27]

Besides hearing the confessions of the many who came, Gibault baptized seven children and one adult, an Indian girl, aged twenty-two. Also, he conferred the nuptial blessing on one couple, a French-Canadian trader, Gabriel Côte, and his Indian wife, Agathe Desjardins. Recording the event in the parish register, Gibault wrote that the couple had, on August 17, 1765, given mutual consent in the presence of witnesses, ". . . promising, as they could not do otherwise, owing to the absence of a priest, to take advantage of the arrival of the first one, to have their marriage validated and thus legitimize a child born on February 28, 1767."[28] During the French regime, such marriages, at first encouraged, were later frowned upon because it was discovered by experience that too often the progeny of such unions acquired the worst features of each ethnic group. When the English came into possession of Canada they followed the same policy. An official complaint regarding the wedding witnessed by Gibault at Michilimackinac was registered with Bishop Briand who informed Gibault: ". . . you solemnized a marriage . . . of a Frenchman and an Indian woman which displeased the government. . . . I excused you on the grounds that you might not know the discipline at this point. . . . Be careful not to do it again. . . ."[29]

At Michilimackinac Father Gibault was still a good 200 leagues from his destination. Leaving the scene of his first apostolic labors on July 28, 1768, or shortly thereafter, he traveled the length of Lake Michigan along its eastern shore to the mouth of the St. Joseph River and up that stream a short distance to

Fort St. Joseph. There he stopped for a day or two, at least long enough to perform seven baptisms. One of the children baptized was the offspring of Timothé Boucher de Montbrun and his wife Therésè Archange Gibault, the missionary's first cousin.[30] Taking to his canoe again, the priest followed the St. Joseph River to its confluence with the Kankakee. On it and the Des Plaines he reached the historic Illinois River which took him to Kaskaskia. On arrival, probably no earlier than late September, the missionary was welcomed joyously. He informed Briand: "I have been better received than I could have hoped, judging by the sorrow at my being able to remain in but one place, for all desired to have me reside among them."[31]

After hastily visiting all of the French villages, the new pastor determined to make Kaskaskia his headquarters, explaining to his superior: "I have found myself constrained for many reasons to choose Kaskaskia as my residence because the Kaskaskians are the ones who sent a petition to Your Grace to which you replied by a letter addressed to Father Meurin in which you promised them a curé; and because Kaskaskia is the most populous village."[32] Once settled, Gibault must have expected to launch himself vigorously into his apostolate. However, he was promptly stricken with an annoyingly protracted bout of fever, an affliction from which nearly all immigrants to the Illinois Country suffered soon after their arrival. Father Meurin reported to Bishop Briand: "M. Gibault since his arrival in this country has been nearly always sick with fever, at first high and dangerous, and then slight and slow, against which his courage has always upheld him so that he was able to perform his principal functions in the parish of the Immaculate Conception at Kaskaskia where he judged it best to take up residence."[33] Pierre Gibault need not have fretted at his momentary incapacity. Had he but known, three decades and more of apostolic labors in the Mississippi Valley lay before him.

V

---

## APOSTOLATE 1768-1778

Establishing headquarters at Kaskaskia, where he settled
his mother and sister in a dwelling adjacent to his quarters, Father Pierre Gibault certainly contacted Father Sebastien Meurin,
promptly ascertaining the manner in which the newly arrived
priest and his elder confrere would share out the pastoral care
of their vast mission. Perhaps the old veteran missionary would
be a severe taskmaster. Much to Gibault's relief, Father Meurin,
who was, actually, Gibault's superior, declared his wish to assume the role of assistant. He desired, he said, to convey to
Gibault whatever information he had of the area's religious condition ". . . so that at my death he would know all. . . ."[1] To in-

duce people to accept Gibault as their official pastor, Meurin retired to Prairie du Rocher whose twenty-four souls

> . . . invited me to finish my days with them, promising me to build a rectory and to furnish me everything I needed for the remainder of my life, no matter what infirmity might befall me. I promised . . . not to abandon them save by main force, reserving . . . the right to go and help in the other villages as much as I could according to their needs, and leaving to their church after my death all I had from them or from other sources, if no more Jesuits returned to the country. They supplied me with a domestic and a horse and buggy for my journeys, undoubtedly so that they might have me the longer. May the divine goodness keep account of their deeds![2]

Sebastien Meurin was lavish in his praise of his new colleague, writing to Bishop Briand: "M. Gibault is full of ardor, and because of this he will not last long if he is [left] alone and often has to go on hard journeys . . . unless it pleases God to renew His ancient miracles. . . . He has had the good fortune to have almost everyone in these two parishes make their Easter duty, which some have neglected for many years."[3] Pierre Gibault, however, was sharply critical of his elder associate. He reported his first impressions thus:

> Father Meurin is sixty-six years old, broken in health and often marked by absent-mindedness, and even more by avarice and self-interest, which do him great harm; otherwise he is of good habits and very zealous. I reported to him what people said about him, and he told me that he was on the verge of his second childhood, and would be abandoned by everybody in the country. However, this will not be the case, for I will shelter him myself, and take all possible care of him. We are, and I hope that we always shall be, on good terms, although I disregard most of his counsels, because he is too much inclined to severity and wishes to accomplish everything by force. On my arrival in this village there were not more than ten men who had received Communion in four years, for the sole reason that they did not want to confess to a Jesuit. I am trying with all my might to divest them of this evil prejudice.[4]

44

Six months later Gibault received a reply from his bishop who commented regarding Father Meurin:

> You must look twice before you go against the advice of
> Father Meurin and you must mistrust your own lights; his way of
> writing and of rendering account to me does not show a man gone
> back to infancy. One must not be prejudiced nor beguiled by men
> not very Christian, such as you have depicted to me before and
> now depict again. It is never good to give way to harshness, but
> often this name is given to firmness; and the laxity which aban-
> dons the interests of God is called prudence; but it is only pru-
> dence of the flesh, the enemy of God . . . follow my counsels . . .
> they keep to the happy mean.[5]

The objective fact of the matter may well have been that Gibault's criticism of the aging Father Meurin was partially correct, but for reasons quite misunderstood by Gibault. Meurin had witnessed the brutal and precipitate destruction of the Immaculate Conception Indian mission near Kaskaskia, a cruel ending of nearly a century of quite successful missionary effort by his fellow Jesuits. Most painful to him, undoubtedly, was the wanton demolition of the mission chapel and the heartless desecration of the cemetery where lay the remains of many Jesuits who had given their all for the betterment of the Indians. Meurin unquestionably hoped against hope that the Jesuits would soon return to resume their apostolate. In the meantime, he stood by, a helpless witness, while, to his horror, Catholic Frenchmen scandalously ravished the chapel, alienating its furnishings, and even its sacred vessels, to profane use. Wounded to the quick, Meurin cried out against such sacrilege, demanding at least the restoration of the altar plate to its proper religious use. He wrote to Bishop Briand:

> For myself, I ask nothing—I am too old. But I shall always see
> with grief the chapel and the cemetery profaned to serve as a
> garden and storehouse by the English who rent them from M.
> Jean Baptiste Beauvais . . . The vestment cases and sacred vessels

are now in his apartments as well as the windows, the altar, and the floor, etc. The continual reproaches I make him on that score keep him alienated from me and have kept him from the sacraments for three years. I beg you to give me a decision on this, and say whether, . . . he can be granted absolution and be exempt from handing over the said articles to the parish church: that is my whole request.[6]

Those who complained to Gibault about the old missionary naturally portrayed him as an avaricious, unbending, doddering old man, confused in mind, petty, and very childish. While Gibault apparently arrived at some sort of compromise with Beauvais, very little of a practical nature could be done about the whole matter as was also the case regarding the land at Cahokia claimed by the priests of the Missions-Etrangères.

On June 22, 1722, these priests were granted by the crown a concession of land at Cahokia, four leagues square with frontage on the Mississippi River.[7] Over the years these missionaries erected a rectory of stone, a mill, and other suitable structures. On November 5, 1763, when the Jesuits were about to depart from the Illinois Country, the abbé François Forget du Verger, in charge of the mission of the Holy Family at Cahokia, sold the concession, without authorization, to Jean Baptiste La Grange, a merchant trader residing at Cahokia. The purchaser agreed to pay 12,500 livres in installments to the Paris headquarters of the Missions-Etrangères.[8] Forthwith, Forget du Verger departed for Paris. On learning of Father Meurin's presence in the Illinois Country, the abbé Boiret, Quebec superior of the Missions-Etrangères, wrote to Meurin, on May 3, 1767, giving him power of attorney, requesting the missionary to recover the property.[9] The missionary presented his documents to the British commandant, Captain Hugh Forbes, who refused to order the property returned, but promised to prevent its changing hands until a ruling was received from General Gage, commander of all British forces in North America.[10] There the matter rested until Gibault arrived.

46

When Father Pierre Gibault came to the Illinois Country, he also brought letters granting him power of attorney respecting the Cahokia property. He could be expected to take a personal interest in the affair since the priests of the Missions-Etrangères had supported him during his seminary training. In March 1770 Gibault reported to the bishop:

> . . . that mission [at Cahokia] formerly so flourishing is nothing any more. . . . the mills are in ruins, the milldams have been carried away by the waters, the barns have fallen, the orchard for lack of a fence has been destroyed by animals . . . in a word, only the four walls of the house are left, for the roof and floors are not worth anything. Furthermore the colonel never would permit me to rent it, giving as his reason that he was keeping it to make a barracks . . . none of the purchasers is in a position or desires to oppose [any efforts] of the authorities of the Seminary to recover the improperly sold property. Thus there is no opposition to the recovery of these estates, except the English.[11]

Gibault pointed out, however, that even if he succeeded in recovering the property he was in no position to supervise restoring or managing it. Hence, if the priests of the seminary wished to regain their property, let them send men to accomplish the objective. And there the matter rested. Nothing now remains of that vast estate except the restored French church and a scattering of badly weathered tombstones in the graveyard surrounding it.

Kaskaskia's new pastor lost no time settling into routine parish work. About six months after his arrival, Gibault reported to Bishop Briand on February 15, 1769:

> I have public prayers in the church every evening at sunset. [I teach] catechism four times a week, thrice for the whites and once for the negroes or slaves. As often as possible I give exhortations on subjects which I believe to be profitable for the instruction of the listeners. In a word, I employ my small talent for the glory of our Saviour, my own sanctification and that of my neighbor, as it seems to me, I ought to do. I hope our Saviour will re-

gard rather what I should like to do and the intention with which
I do it, rather than what I actually accomplish.[12]

Though statistics tabulating the number of sacramental adminis-
trations are by no means a yardstick for measuring a priest's
zeal, they are at least some indication of it. Fortunately, the official records of the parish of the Immaculate Conception at Kaskaskia have survived, almost completely intact.[13] From these one
learns much concerning Gibault's labors for his flock. Between
October 1, 1768, when the newly arrived missionary made his
first baptismal entry, until 1778, he baptized 243 persons.
While the majority were infant children of French parents, there
were also a noticeable number of Indians and Negroes, among
the latter eighteen adults. Perhaps the most satisfying such occasions were those on which the young priest baptized three of his
nieces and a nephew, children of his sister, Marie Louise, who
had accompanied her brother to the Illinois Country and there
married Joseph Nigneau on September 11, 1770.[14]

The marriages solemnized by Father Gibault reveal a great
deal about the people residing in the Illinois Country. Marriages between Negro slaves were witnessed by fellow slaves
with the recorded consent of the owners of the contracting parties. A very few marriages of Indian couples are recorded and
only one union of a Frenchman and an Indian woman. These
two were Antoine Janis and Angelique La Plume, whose tribe,
Gibault noted, was unknown. Weddings contracted between persons of note were recorded in minute detail, giving the place of
origin of the bride and groom and often that of the parents of
each. In his sister's case the pastor noted that the bride, Marie
Louise, was a native of the parish of St. François, government
of Three Rivers, diocese of Quebec, the legitimate daughter of
the late Pierre Gibault and Marie St. Jean. With a proud flour-
ish the priest added that the marriage was solemnized in the
presence of the bride's mother and the pastor, her brother. A
perusal of the marriage records also reveals the increasing in-

flux of English-speaking immigrants. For example, on November 27, 1770, Gibault witnessed the marriage of Jean Langois, a "native of New York in New England" and Marie Willan, "a native of Waterfort in Ireland, daughter of Laurent Willan and Catherine Farrille." Patently, the bride's parents must have been Lawrence Whalen and Catherine Farrell of Waterford.

The presence of native-born Irish in the Mississippi Valley at such an early date is readily explained. Lieutenant Colonel John Wilkins, appointed British commandant of the Illinois Country in the spring of 1768, had, just the previous year, brought out from Ireland a part of the 18th (Royal Irish) Regiment, composed chiefly of Irish recruits. Wilkins may not have looked with any sympathy on things Catholic, but the necessity of controlling five companies of raw Irish recruits must certainly have inclined him to prudence. Since his wild Irishmen would surely respect the priest, the colonel was careful to gain Gibault's friendship and recruit his support. The missionary informed his bishop:

> Our commandant offered me his support and that of his troops if I should need them for our religion. As it is an Irish regiment where there are many Catholics, he has asked me to treat those who are of the faith as I would my parishioners.[15]

Ministering to the troops quickly became more of a burden than was anticipated. Before the soldiers had served a complete year at Kaskaskia over a hundred conscripts and camp followers had died of fever.[16] If Father Gibault had been as careful in recording burials as he was of baptisms and marriages, we could have learned much of interest regarding the soldiers serving at Kaskaskia. However, the burial records during Gibault's first ten years at Kaskaskia are obviously incomplete, showing large gaps which will never be filled.[17]

During the early years of his apostolate at Kaskaskia, Father Gibault was understandably greatly appreciated by his people who showed themselves most grateful for his presence. In time, however, subtle changes of attitude began to appear. The French, accustomed, previous to France's loss of the territory, to having the crown bear the financial burden of supporting the church and the clergy, now learned that they must assume that obligation themselves, accepting a system of tithing.[18] When, of necessity, Father Meurin sought to introduce tithing, he was bitterly criticized by the people who accused him of avarice and self-interest. At the beginning of Gibault's pastorate the parishioners spontaneously contributed their tithes.[19] Later, when they realized that their pastor would be absent frequently caring for the neighboring French villages and distant posts, they objected to donating on the grounds that the priest did not devote his full time to Kaskaskia. The opposition came into the open over Gibault's determination to erect a new church to replace the crumbling structure erected by the Jesuits in 1740.[20] In spite of staunch opposition the young pastor succeeded in building a new church, even a quite pretentious one, which served the parish until 1838.[21]

Notwithstanding the opposition of his Kaskaskia parishioners, Pierre Gibault routinely visited Cahokia and Prairie du Rocher, when illness prevented Father Meurin from adequately caring for his people, as well as the newly founded St. Louis and Ste. Genevieve, both on the west bank of the Mississippi in Spanish territory. Though Rocheblave, commandant for the Spanish at Ste. Genevieve, had peremptorily banished Father Meurin, his attitude toward Gibault was much more conciliatory. This temporizing commandant's change of heart was partially explained by Gibault who informed Bishop Briand: "I have, however, always officiated at Ste. Genevieve, which is two leagues distant from my parish on the other bank of the Mississippi and consequently belongs to the Spaniards. I gained with ease the permission of the English governor [to go there]; and the Spanish commandant, being very devout, would have liked me to be there always."[22] Possibly Rocheblave was already beginning to have his doubts regarding the ability of the Spanish to maintain permanent control of their portion of the Illinois Country. Probably more cogently, however, on June 18, 1770, the Spanish commandant became the proud father of a son. Who would baptize the child if not Father Gibault whose ecclesiastical jurisdiction came from the bishop of Quebec whom Rocheblave had only a few years previously refused to recognize. Be that as it may, the following entry appears in the baptismal record of the parish at Ste. Genevieve:

> The 27th of May, 1771, by us the undersigned priest Vicar General of his Lordship the Bishop of Quebec for the Illinois Country were supplied the ceremonies of Holy Baptism to Pierre born the 18th of June of the past year of the legitimate marriage of Monsieur Philippe François Marquis de Rocheblave and of Dame Marie Michel Dufrêne his wife. The godfather was Don Pedro Pernas Captain of the Infantry and Lieutenant Governor for His Catholic Majesty for the Illinois Country and its dependencies and the godmother was Dame Felicite Robino de Portneuf wife of the godfather, for whom Dame Marianne Billeron wife of Sr. Vallée captain of the militia and Judge of Ste. Genevieve has taken the place in her absence and have signed with us as also the father who was present.
>
> Gibault Ptre Vc. Gl.
>
> Pedro Piernas
> Marianne Billeron
> Rocheblave                                                Vallé[23]

Making regular visits to the French villages on either side of the Mississippi in the vicinity of Kaskaskia, though time consuming, was not too physically trying for the young Father Gibault. However these journeys did not fulfill his obligation to care for such outlying posts as the distant Vincennes, the fort at St. Joseph, and the several Indian villages in between. Vincennes was the first of these to claim the priest's attention within the first year of his apostolate. Over a year before Gibault reached Kaskaskia, Phillibert, lay church warden at Vincennes, forwarded a pathetic plea to the prelate at Quebec, begging the bishop to send a missionary.[24] Two years later, when, in the meantime, no missionary reached Vincennes, sixteen of the townsfolk again petitioned Bishop Briand:

> We can give you only a very faint idea of the misfortunes which the lack of religion brings upon us since we have been deprived of priests who formerly cared for this parish. [Among these] is the sad state and wretched disorder which too much license can cause among children who have no fear of their own fathers, living in ignorance and abandoning themselves to everything sensual that youth is capable of, and always avoiding the path of virtue; with these are joined the thousand other bad consequences that come to people who are without faith because deprived of opportunities to perform their Christian duties. . . . Wherefore we cannot too strongly place before you the danger which threatens us if we are abandoned by the Almighty and above all by our faithful pastors . . . we hope that you will heed the plea of loyal citizens of your diocese, and that you will heed our plea for a priest who will set us aright and speedily bring us back to God.[25]

When he had been at Kaskaskia for little over a year, Pierre Gibault finally set out to visit Vincennes. The parishioners at Kaskaskia were loath to allow their pastor to attempt the 200-mile overland journey pointing out that not only was he still suffering from the effects of fever but the road to Vincennes was known to be infested with marauding Indians. So real was the danger from savages that the missionary informed Bishop Briand from Vincennes:

> . . . I cannot travel to these places without being liable at any moment to be scalped by the savages. Twenty-two men have been killed or captured, which is worse for they are burned, on the road I passed over, since I have been in Illinois, but at different times. So when I went away, it was in spite of my village, which several times assembled itself to oppose my departure. I took, however, for prudence, ten men with me, and I shall have twenty to go back.[26]

52

On this first of several missionary journeys to Vincennes, Father Gibault was received as an angel from heaven. He described his welcome thus:

> . . . upon my arrival all the people came in crowds to receive me at the shore of the Wabash river. Some threw themselves on their knees without being able to speak, others spoke only with sobs; some cried, "My father, save us, we are at the edge of hell;" others said, "God has not forsaken us yet, for it is He who sends you to us to make us repent our sins." Some said, "Oh sir, why did you not come a month ago? Then my poor wife, my dear father, my dear mother, my poor child would not have died without the sacraments."[27]

Gibault remained at Vincennes for nearly two months, supplying the ceremonies perforce omitted by the pious churchwarden, Phillibert, for all of those who had been baptized or married since the departure, in 1763, of the last Jesuit missionary to care for Vincennes. Also, he induced the people to repair and enlarge their log church which was erected in 1749, when Father Meurin was stationed at the post.[28] From 1770 forward Gibault visited Vincennes regularly every second year, as entries signed by him in the parish records prove.[29]

As the only physically vigorous priest in the Mississippi Valley, it fell to Pierre Gibault to undertake extended missionary tours to such distant posts as Peoria, St. Joseph, Miami, Ouiatanon, and even Michilimackinac. Considering his many obligations in the Kaskaskia area alone, it speaks highly of the man's zeal to notice that between January 1773 and May 1776 he undertook two very lengthy voyages. Besides the obvious physical exertions associated with these arduous journeys, there existed very real danger from the aborigines. Elaborating on that threat, Gibault explained to his superior, on June 20, 1772:

> I have nothing new to tell you except that we are constantly exposed, and now more than ever, to the danger of being massacred by the Indians from the countries of the lower Mississippi

on which our village borders. Other villages are exempt from the danger. Since I last wrote you, more than twenty people have been slain. I was taken three times by the Indians. Each time they let me go, but forbade me to tell anyone about it. I obeyed them because if it were known I should never again be allowed to travel about, and because, if the Indians were discovered through me, and I were ever recaptured, I should never be set free. I have adopted the plan of carrying no fire arms, for fear of being tempted to use them and thus having myself killed, or inspiring them with the fear of being killed and that they would anticipate me instead of taking me prisoner.[30]

Possibly Gibault was persuaded to make the first of these excursions, in 1773, because at least a portion of his vast parish was removed from his care with the arrival of Father Hilaire de Genoveaux, a French Capuchin, whom Spanish officials sent to be resident pastor at Ste. Genevieve with at least unofficial responsibility for all Catholics residing along the western bank of the Mississippi.[31]

Leaving Kaskaskia in the dead of winter, Gibault reached Vincennes in January 1773, where he baptized some children and witnessed a marriage. Then he set out for the little trading post of St. Joseph near the mouth of the St. Joseph River, 235 miles to the north. Arriving in March, the traveling apostle baptized two children on March 7 and presided at a burial on March 21.[32] The missionary's next port of call was Michilimackinac, 350 miles to the north and east. With luck and fair weather Gibault could have reached his destination in about twelve days for the French voyageurs could travel ten leagues, or a bit over thirty miles a day, in good weather and on fresh water such as Lake Michigan. All one knows for certain of Gibault's apostolic work there is one lone record of a marriage he witnessed between sieur Hyacinthe Amelin, a trader, and Marie Joseph Maingans on June 28, 1773.[33] If we are to judge from Gibault's activity during his previous visit, in the summer of 1768 when he was en route to the Illinois Country, the missionary must

54

have been very busy hearing confessions and the like. This season was the most propitious for both trader and missionary for it was during the summer that the Indians came in to trade at the post as well as when supplies for the coming winter were freighted up from Montreal. In all likelihood the visiting missionary was again importuned to remain permanently at Michilimackinac, but, of course, he was obliged to return to Kaskaskia, a wearisome journey of 800 miles.

During the five years Pierre Gibault had resided at Kaskaskia disturbing changes had come to pass. Adapting themselves to the rule of their new British masters would have been difficult enough for the French citizenry if their rulers had given them some sort of civil government. Instead, they were governed by a succession of military commandants, the last of whom, Wilkins, besides being a petty tyrant was not noted for his honesty. Adding to the confusion was the influx of noteworthy numbers of English-speaking Americans, especially businessmen, who neither spoke French nor were in sympathy with their neighbors whom, perhaps, they disdained. When shrewd Yankee traders began controlling trade, Frenchmen soon banded together against them for mutual protection. In 1772, when the British garrison was withdrawn, except a small troop of fifty men under the command of Captain Hugh Lord, public order and morality rapidly degenerated. In the midst of this unrest the pastor, once generally liked and respected, soon became the focal point of resentment for he inveighed against disorder, immorality, and laxity. Criticism of their pastor, for the most part unjustified, soon took the form of the typical French appeal to bureaucracy. Traders going to Montreal carried letters to the bishop of Quebec from people at Kaskaskia complaining that their pastor was absent too much, that he showed favoritism, or gave reason for people to be surprised at his manner of life. Besides, there were rumors of war drifting in from across the mountains to the east. Perhaps the seaboard colonies might revolt. If that happened, what effect would it have in the Mississippi Valley? If the Americans won, what would happen? Would the new masters suppress Catholicism and demand that all the old French ways be abandoned? By nature independent and outspoken, Father Gibault expressed himself forcefully, opposing misconduct. By 1775, when he set off on his second lengthy missionary tour, Kaskaskia and the Illinois Country had ceased to be for him the ideal field for his apostolate which it had been five years before.

Departing from Kaskaskia soon after New Year's, 1775, Father Gibault spent some days at Vincennes where, in February 1775, he administered the sacraments of baptism and matrimony.[34] He must certainly have done likewise at St. Joseph, but he left no record of his passing. Pushing on to Michilimackinac, the harried priest seems to have spent much of the month of June 1775 ministering to the people.[35] Then he took the opportunity to visit Montreal.[36] Perhaps this journey was undertaken only to inform his sisters that his mother was quite ill and not expected to live, a sad fact he learned from a letter which had reached him in May.[37] Some have conjectured that Gibault went on to Quebec to report to Bishop Briand. One might hope that he did so, if only to defend himself, but the surmise has no documentary foundation. By October 3, 1775, the priest was back at the northern post of Michilimackinac for on that day he baptized the infant daughter of John Askin, the king's commissioner at the post.[38] Told that a boat bound for the Illinois Country was momentarily expected, Gibault remained at Michilimackinac awaiting it. In the meantime he apparently reflected on his situation. In Montreal he had learned of the outbreak of the American Revolution as well as Bishop Briand's resounding exhortation urging Canadians to remain loyal to the British crown.[39] What would all of this mean to Father Gibault except more trouble and discontent? Should he return to Kaskaskia or should he request a change of location?

56

On October 9, 1775, Pierre Gibault composed a letter to his bishop:

> For the last eight years I have obeyed you, firmly believing that in doing so I was obeying God himself. This is my fourth expedition, the shortest of which is 500 leagues in length, visiting, exhorting, reforming, as best I can, the people you have confided to me, employing not only what the writings of the missionaries taught but reminding the long-time residents of the customs they instituted at each place. I tried to conform to those uses in each place in so far as I could discover them. Nothing deterred me from my duty: neither suffering nor illness nor fatigue nor rain nor snow nor ice nor heat nor winds nor storms nor hunger nor danger from the Indians. I have never complained to you even though for four years I have not had so much as a bottle of wine for my table or any of life's other small comforts. Furthermore, I have never been envious of the lot of others.
>
> But now my body is weakened by these sufferings and I can no longer accomplish what both you and I would wish. I am now forty years old.[40] Never sparing myself, I have often had poor food and frequently went hungry, traveling on foot day and night, exposed to all sorts of weather and in every season. Worst of all is the mental anxiety, being a stranger in a country of libertines, exposed to all the calumnies which the irreligious and impious could invent, having my every action, even the most well-intentioned, misinterpreted and misrepresented to you. In spite of my care [of them], my weariness, my solicitude and even the 4,000 livres, and more, I contributed toward building a new church, which I never made the least effort [to have erected], but which was [built after a vote of a] general assembly. Yet I am in debt to the amount I mentioned. But I encounter such ingratitude that, for the most part, no one offers to contribute, even those who daily squander [money] for drink and debauchery. For all of these and other reasons, I ask you to let me leave the Illinois. . . . The people have lost what they had when M. Forget and the Jesuit Father Aubert thought they had never seen a better place. After the suppression of the Society [of Jesus] Father Meurin suffered and is still suffering a veritable martyrdom. It would be sinful on my part if I did not tell you . . . that I cannot any longer condone that Babylon. . . .

Do not imagine, Monseigneur, that I am motivated by self interest. . . . My sister is solidly established in Illinois. I received a letter in May informing me that my mother was then suffering from a malady judged to be fatal. I am, therefore, alone now and any place is the same to me. Still one must be useful somewhere. You are, after all, my father, my judge, my bishop. If you decide to order me to return, I will go. My primary duty is to obey. . . .

Your most humble, submissive

At Michilimackinac and obedient servant,

October 9, 1775. P. Gibault, priest, missionary.[41]

Between the lines of this discouraged communication one senses Gibault's wearied, puzzled, injured spirit. Could he cope with the difficulties he knew disturbed times would bring? His people were changing with the times, but not, it seemed, for the better. Perhaps he was the wrong man in the wrong place at the wrong time. Would he not serve the Illinois Country best by simply withdrawing? Nonetheless, if his superior directed him to continue there, he would return, even though very reluctantly.

The next communication Bishop Briand received from his troubled subject was a letter written by Father Gibault at Detroit:

Though I had the honor of writing you from Michilimackinac, finding an unexpected courier [leaving for Canada] from Detroit, . . . I take the occasion to send you my humble respects and to repeat what I already wrote from Michilimackinac. I inform you that, reaching that post in September, I stayed there until November 4, awaiting the assured arrival of a boat, which was already expected when I arrived from Montreal. Realizing, finally, that I was waiting in vain, I was obliged to settle in for the winter. Faced with that unpleasant alternative, I preferred risking disaster on Lake Huron to spending the winter there [at Michilimackinac]. Hence, I set out in a small bark canoe accompanied by one man and a child, both of whom were making their first trip. I, myself, have little skill with boats, having made the trip only once before, sixteen years ago. Then I slept every night as well as much of the day so that I knew nothing about the dangerous places which are frequent in this wretched craft. Guiding

58

the canoe myself through ice, snow, eight inches deep in level country, winds and storms, I reached Detroit in twenty-two days. In the living memory of man, no one has ever made the trip in that season. I have been here for ten days. Before my arrival the river froze over and can be crossed as is done from Quebec to Levis in winter. Thus, I am detained here. I may get away this winter, but perhaps, as the old-timers tell me, not before March. God only knows. The suffering I endured coming here from Michilimackinac has so numbed me that I am barely aware of disappointment at being unable to return to the Illinois. I shall do all I can to be useful at Detroit, relieving the two venerable old men in charge here.

Besides, my Lord, I shall profit by the delay to make a longer retreat than I could have done anywhere else, since I have no duties here. Father Potier tells me that the Hurons all asked me to stay with them, learn their language and be a second father to them. They came to me at his home to salute me ceremoniously. I report this in passing, preferring to return to Canada rather than staying at Detroit. . . . Nothing would please me more than to learn that you enjoy perfect health and that you are recalling me from the Illinois. . . . I beg you to inform me of your latest plans. I remain, with profound respect, my Lord,

At Detroit                Your humble and very obedient servant,
December 4, 1775.      P. Gibault, priest.[42]

During Father Gibault's year's absence from his post, Bishop Briand, understandably concerned regarding the serious complaints he received, determined to investigate. He wrote to Father Meurin, requesting a frank opinion.[43] The troubled old missionary replied on May 23, 1776:

I have been waiting patiently for M. Gibault's return. He arrived today, May 22, full of indignation at his parish which he absolutely wishes to abandon as soon as he can arrange his affairs. If he had continued as he began, following the advice which you and I gave him, he would not be unhappy. During his first years he was loved, esteemed, and sought after. In response [to criticism he says] he is free [to act as he wishes], forgetting that he is a priest and a vicar general. He took to participating in games with

59

the young men, proving his skill, agility, strength etc. He became too familiar with the ladies, pleased at arousing jealousies among them, visiting and conversing lengthily [with them] . . . [also, he is given to] late hours, card playing, celebrating and the like. He showed inebriates that he could drink as much or more than they. Over the last five or six years he has lost his reputation and the respect [of the people]. However, he says, and perhaps believes, that he is blameless. According to him, it is the people who are at fault. But they say he has not maintained the proprieties of his position. I learned all of this only lately. He flatly denied everything. But during his recent absence I discovered that they are only too true. God grant that he is better received and that he profits by the advice you gave him. I will not fail to inform you, immediately, about his conduct. I love this poor country too much to neglect its ills. . . . The people of this country are neither better nor worse than those in Canada. They are more good than bad. I have proved this as did all my predecessors. Though one tongue maligned us, a hundred others defended us. This is my constant consolation as it was that of our [Jesuits] and of MM. Thaumur, Mercier, Gagnon, Laurent, very worthy priests of the diocese whose memory is still held in benediction in this country.[44]

That Pierre Gibault did not comport himself with the reserve and dignity which both Meurin and Briand considered proper for a priest is quite probably true. It is to be remembered, however, that both the bishop and the aging missionary were products of the rigid ecclesiastical tradition of France where both were born and received the whole of their sacerdotal training. Easy familiarity with the people would be judged by them to be improper. Gibault, however, a native Canadian, who knew the frontier and its people, evidently found the accepted tradition uncomfortable, perhaps even impossible. His brief seminary career left little time for training in ecclesiastical manners. Perhaps, too, his bent of character was such that he could not bring himself to embrace the pattern of conduct proposed. Perhaps some of the people were more than surprised at Gibault's easy relationship with his people. Obviously some complained to the bishop. It would seem rather narrow-minded of them to criticize their pastor for taking recreation with the young men of the village. Lacking any sacerdotal companions, it would be rather natural for Gibault to associate with his own age group. Maybe the French never before saw a priest take part in athletics, but also they had never before been given as pastor a man whose background, previous to his ordination, was of a piece with their own. As for Father Gibault's dealings with the fair sex, Father Meurin's remarks on the subject may well have been applied to himself or to any priest in similar circumstances. Pious ladies are all too prone to compete for sacerdotal attention. Objectively, it would be fair to conclude that Gibault was not quite reasonably chided for conduct hardly blameworthy, or at very worst somewhat lacking in restraint. It should be pointed out that Gibault was not chided because he neglected his duties to his people. If some of his more Jansenistic parishioners found his social behavior not to their liking, at least they did not complain that he neglected them.

Complaints regarding Father Gibault's conduct, once launched, did not cease. A little less than a year after his return to Kaskaskia Bishop Briand wrote him, on April 26, 1777:

> My poor son, you began well, causing me to shed tears of joy. But now I weep in bitter sadness. Try to repair the scandal and revive within you the grace of the priesthood which you received by the imposition of my hands. I am not shocked by your failures; the fickleness of the human heart is as great as its inconstancy. The dangers you face are overwhelming and continual. We are not protected if we do not use the weapons which our Lord taught us: Watch and pray. . . . I find myself obliged in conscience to send you a visitor. . . . I will be delighted to find you innocent or repentant or open to correction. . . .[45]

Before the visitor, really an ecclesiastical investigator, reached the Illinois Country, Father Sebastien Meurin, Gibault's only associate on the east bank of the Mississippi, died on February

23, 1777. Now Gibault was truly alone. His relations with the bishop hardly improved. In the one letter to that superior surviving from the year 1777, Gibault explained the details of an altercation involving himself and Despains, the trader with whom he came to Kaskaskia in 1768. That the missionary more than half expected less than a sympathetic hearing is evident from his request that his opponent be not heard at the episcopal court. He wrote, in part:

> I am writing you this because he [Despains] is writing to you. As he is interpreter for the king, I do not at all doubt that he will make use of some influence. I beg you to send this entire matter back to me as your Vicar General, and as having knowledge of things both public and private. . . . Otherwise I shall have scarcely any authority in this wretched land.[46]

What decision Bishop Briand rendered regarding Father Gibault's request is unknown. However, it is indicative that the visitor whom the bishop sent, Father Jean-François Hubert, set out for the Illinois Country just a few months after Gibault's letter reached Quebec. Before the visitor reached Kaskaskia George Rogers Clark had captured the town on July 4, 1778. With that change of fortune Father Gibault's whole subsequent career was changed also.

---

PIERRE GIBAULT

AND GEORGE ROGERS CLARK

As many historians of the American Revolution agree, George Rogers Clark's daring capture of Kaskaskia, on July 4, 1778, was of significant importance in determining the initial boundary of the United States at the Treaty of Paris in 1783. Precisely what part Pierre Gibault played in Clark's striking success has long been debated. John Law, in his *Colonial History of Vincennes*, published in 1858, declared, unequivocally, that to Gibault ". . . next to Clark and Vigo the United States are [more] indebted for the accession of the states comprised in what was the original Northwest Territory than to any other man."[1] Others, however, such as Alvord in the introduction to his *Kaskaskia Records*, seem to hold that Gibault was actually a retiring temporizer ". . . ready to use his influence with the people, but preferred to throw the responsibility on others, so that, if the issue should be different from what was anticipated, he would still be able to use the argument to the British authorities, which we find that he actually put forward in 1786."[2] Since this incident in Father Gibault's life is by far the most interesting, if not also the most important, any biography of the man must study it at some depth.

How Pierre Gibault, long the lone missionary in the Illinois Country, became involved in the revolt of the American colonies against George III requires some brief review of the importance of the West to both the British and American protagonists. In spite of the British Proclamation of October 7, 1763, expressly forbidding it, Americans began to settle beyond the Atlantic watershed in the area specifically designated by the British as an Indian reserve. In face of such harrowing experiences as Indian attacks during Pontiac's conspiracy, little clusters of frontier cabins continued to spring up even as far westward as the Kentucky River. At the outbreak of our Revolution, both the British and the Americans realized the strategic value of the West. If the British could induce the Indians to attack the Americans from their western rear, the Continental army might be obliged to divert strong forces from the eastern seaboard, thus weakening its none too effective strength. As for the Americans, if they could recruit the trans-Allegheny tribes as allies, or even render them reasonably neutral, much would be gained. To accomplish that objective it became essential to gain control, somehow, of the almost completely unsettled country north of the Ohio River, the breeding ground of the Indian marauders. But within the vast triangle formed by the Ohio, the Mississippi, and the Great Lakes lay several large settlements of former French subjects who, since 1763, had been under the military rule of George III. To win effectively in the West, conquest of these French villages, especially Detroit, was obviously essential. Though the Continental Congress understood its importance, men and money to launch such a campaign were practically unavailable. If, then, the frontiersmen sympathetic to the Revolution were to avoid annihilation at the hands of British troops and their Indian allies, those hardy folk must rely on themselves. This, the American frontier citizens prepared to do under the effective leadership of George Rogers Clark.

Born on November 19, 1752, near Charlottesville, Albemarle County, Virginia, Clark, who learned surveying from an uncle, came into the Ohio Valley in 1772 in the practice of his profession. In 1774, at the outbreak of Lord Dunmore's War against the Shawnee, Clark served under Captain Michael Cresap, whose father, Thomas, was one of the leaders of the Ohio Land Company. In 1775 Clark was employed by that company as a deputy surveyor along the Kentucky River. In the course of his work, Clark discovered that Judge Richard Henderson and his North Carolina associates of the Transylvania Company were encroaching on territories claimed by the Ohio Company. Returning to Williamsburg in 1776, Clark induced Patrick Henry, governor of Virginia, to constitute settlements on the Kentucky River a county of Virginia. At the same time the young surveyor obtained a major's commission in the Virginia militia and assumed responsibility for defending the settlers residing in the newly established county.

Aggressive by nature, Major Clark laid plans, through 1777, for the subjugation of the country north of the Ohio, including the French villages found there, especially Detroit. In the spring of 1777 he sent Samuel Moore and Benjamin Linn, disguised as casual hunters, to Kaskaskia and Vincennes for the purpose of assessing their military strength as well as to discover the attitude of the people toward the American cause.[3] Though Clark's spies failed to contact certain known supporters of the Americans at Kaskaskia, they gathered sufficient information to demonstrate that, since 1772, the place was devoid of military protection. That year General Gage ordered the destruction of Fort Chartres and the withdrawal of British troops, except fifty men posted at Kaskaskia under the command of Captain Hugh Lord whom the people generally admired. Four years later, on May 1, 1776, Lord and his troops were recalled to Detroit, leaving Kaskaskia in the hands of Philippe François de Rastel, chevalier de Rocheblave, who had, sometime after 1770, abjured his allegiance to Spain, removed from Ste. Genevieve to Kaskaskia and, supposedly, became a British subject.[4] Hence, the military defense of Kaskaskia rested solely on the shoulders of the local adult male population, possibly 250 men, of whom about 50 were of Anglo-Saxon stock. How many of these would, in case of an attack, follow Rocheblave was a moot question, considering his unpopularity.

The politically vacillating Rocheblave exercised his questionable authority at Kaskaskia so arbitrarily that both French and English resented him. He insisted on receiving from the people every mark of respect once accorded to French commandants, who had represented the crown of France to the French in Illinois. Though no document from British authority designated him to the office, he assumed the position of civil judge as well as military commandant. To the Anglo-Saxons, he denied the civil rights common to citizens under British law, informing them that only French law pertained at Kaskaskia.[5] He governed the French as though he possessed medieval seignorial rights over them. French merchants, however, were favored over their non-French competitors to such an outrageous extent that bitter complaints were forwarded to General Guy Carleton, British governor of Canada.[6] Thus, though a faction of Kaskaskians might remain loyal to George III, perhaps many of the more important citizens were unquestionably disaffected. As for the people at large, fifteen years of British military rule could hardly have engendered any lasting attachment to the English since those years brought neither civic nor economic stability. Yet the average habitant had learned at his mother's knee to detest the New England colonists who, since early in Canada's history, had constantly threatened the French, raiding their villages, inciting the Indians to massacre them, and universally showing contempt for the Catholic religion. Probably the vast majority of the French at Kaskaskia, if they knew anything about the revolt of the British colonies, looked up the *Bostonais* as ". . . notorious rebels that ought to be subdued."[7]

Unknown to the French in the Mississippi Valley, George Rogers Clark was diligently preparing, throughout 1777, the conquest of that area. Having led several retaliatory expeditions against Indian tribes, whose marauding was said to have been instigated by the British, Clark concluded that the only effective defense of the American settlements was the conquest of the whole of what came to be called the Old Northwest. Returning to Williamsburg in October 1777, Clark persuaded Governor Henry to authorize a punitive expedition aimed chiefly at the Illinois Country. After consultation with his council, the governor, on January 2, 1778, issued public orders to Clark authorizing him to muster seven companies of fifty men each for the defense of the county of Kentucky. Secret orders, issued the same day, directed Clark, now a lieutenant colonel, to attack the British post at Kaskaskia.[8] Hastening westward, Clark, after recruiting only 150 men, proceeded to the Falls of the Ohio where he was joined by only a few more troops instead of the four companies he expected to meet him. While encamped there, Clark joyfully learned of France's alliance with the Americans. That diplomatic coup, he was certain, would prove invaluable in winning the support of the French residing in the Illinois Country. On June 24, 1778, Clark, accompanied by 175 men, traveled by boat down the Ohio to the mouth of the Tennessee where he left his crafts and set out overland to Kaskaskia, about 120 miles to the northwest.

It would be a mistake to assume that throughout the spring and summer of 1778 Kaskaskia continued the even tenor of its ways, oblivious of the military danger threatening it. Not only were the Indians known to be restless, but the Americans at Kaskaskia, Daniel and William Murray, Thomas Bentley, Patrick Kennedy, Richard Winston, and others, were rightly suspected of furnishing information to George Morgan, Indian agent for the Americans at Fort Pitt. Rocheblave, himself, was nearly captured by Captain James Willing, early in 1778, when that American military leader was carrying out his daring raid against the British posts on the lower Mississippi.[9] Soon after learning of Willing's presence in the area, Rocheblave's runners informed him of another American force, led by Clark, which was advancing down the Ohio. Convinced that this party was bound for Kaskaskia, Rocheblave summoned all his townspeople to arms.[10] When time passed without any sign of Clark's forces appearing on the Mississippi, the village militia was allowed to stand down. On July 4, 1778, the very day Clark attacked Kaskaskia, Rocheblave wrote a lengthy letter to Guy Carleton warning: "We are upon the eve of seeing here a numerous band of brigands who will establish a chain of communications which will not be easy to break once formed. . . . You have no time to lose to prevent this misfortune."[11]

And, indeed, the British commandant of Kaskaskia was only too correct. Before dusk that afternoon Clark's little band of 175 men was bivouacked not a mile above Kaskaskia. Under cover of darkness, Clark, with a part of his forces, audaciously marched into the town and occupied the small fort while others of his troops created hair-raising diversions throughout the village.[12] Rocheblave was apprehended within the fort and Kaskaskia fell into Clark's hands without a shot being fired in anger. Before the night was over the town was disarmed and the people warned that anyone attempting to escape would be summarily shot. Thus, with only a handful of troops and no reserve to call

68

upon, Clark suddenly found himself victor of a supposedly hostile town with a population of upwards of a thousand and a possible military strength far superior to his own. Clark's only chance of consolidating his conquest lay in psychological harassment.

Throughout the night and into the morning of July 5 Clark and his men deliberately inflamed the imaginations of the towns- folk, leading them to imagine the worst possible calamities of unrestrained plunder, slaughter, and rapine. Even worse, the conviction arose among the people that, like the Acadians, they were about to be scattered to the four winds and, in the process, families would be separated, the men led into captivity and the women and children left to shift for themselves. In the morning, however, the people realized that whatever their fate they had best face it. If they were to be stripped of everything they pos- sessed, it was better to approach their conqueror and arrange the best terms they could. Hence, Father Gibault and five or six leaders sought and were granted an audience with Colonel Clark. Speaking for all the people, Gibault pleaded for but one favor. Since everyone expected the victor to drive the people from their homes, would the colonel allow the citizens to gather in the church, spending some little time for final farewells?[13] Giving no hint of his plans, Clark coldly dismissed Father Gi- bault, reporting: "I carelessly told him that I had nothing to say to his church that he might go their if he did to inform the peo- ple not to venture out of the town[. T]hey attempted some other conversation but was informed that we was not at leisure. . . ."[14]

After remaining in the church for a considerable time, per- haps while the pastor celebrated Mass, the priest, with the prin- cipal men of the village, returned to thank Clark for his consideration. They sought an extension of his clemency, re- questing that the men be permitted to remain with their families wherever they were sent as well as that the women and children be allowed to carry away some of their clothing and a small store of provisions. The vanquished leaders then explained that their people were quite unacquainted with the nature of the current war. Many, they avowed, favored the Americans as much as they dared and more would have undoubtedly embraced the same opinion if they had only been properly informed. These protestations convinced Clark that the people accepted their conquest and would cooperate with the invading force. Then the American leader showed himself the magnanimous victor.

> I asked them very abruptly whether or not they thought they were speaking to savages that I was certain that they did from the tenor of their conversation did they suppose that we ment to strip the women and children or take the Bread out of ther mouths or that we would condesend to make war on the women and Children or the Church that it was to prevent the effution of innocent blood . . . that caused us to visit them, and not the prospect of Plunder . . . that the King of France had joined the Americans . . . as far as their church all religians would be tolerated in america . . . and to convince them that we ware not savages and Plunderers . . . they Might return to their Families and inform them that they might conduct themselves as utial[15]

Such a wholly unexpected reply from Colonel Clark promptly won the Kaskaskians to his banner. Sorrow and apprehension were suddenly turned to profound joy. No wonder, then, that the church's bell pealed out the intoxicating news and that the citizens gladly abjured their fealty to George III, taking an oath of loyalty to the American government.

With Kaskaskia in his grasp, Clark turned his attention to the other villages in the neighborhood. When the people of Kaskaskia learned that Colonel Clark planned to send a punitive expedition against Cahokia, they forthwith offered to go to that village and effect its submission to the Americans. Pointing out that the people at Cahokia were friends and relatives of those at Kaskaskia, the Kaskaskians assured Clark that they would, themselves, easily induce the people at Cahokia to follow their example. If Clark insisted on sending soldiers to Cahokia, they

begged to be allowed to accompany the expedition so that bloodshed might be avoided. With Clark's consent, a number of men
from Kaskaskia accompanied Major Joseph Bowman with a
small detachment of troops to Cahokia. Showing his complete
confidence in the loyalty of the Kaskaskian, Clark recommended
them to go armed and under command of their own militia
officers. Fired with enthusiasm for the project, the French spent
so much time ". . . equiping themselves to appear at the best
advantage that it was night before the party moved."[16] Reaching
Cahokia on July 6, Bowman and his colorfully dressed French
cohorts readily persuaded the Cahokians to follow the example
of their neighbors at Kaskaskia to the south. The citizens of Cahokia took the oath of allegiance to the American cause on July
8, 1778.[17]

Having occupied the French villages along the Mississippi
from Cahokia to Kaskaskia, Vincennes became Colonel Clark's
next military goal. Capture of that settlement was essential to
his major objective, the subduing of Detroit. Observing Father
Gibault's influence over his flock at Kaskaskia, Clark prudently
consulted the missionary regarding his plan to attack Vincennes,
which was also Gibault's spiritual charge. In a lengthy confer-
ence the priest advised that a military expedition against Vincennes was probably a needless effort. He was confident that,
when the inhabitants of Vincennes were acquainted with the
happy outcome of Clark's capture of Kaskaskia, their reaction
would be similar. Clark reported that the missionary declared:
". . . if it was agreable to me he would take this business on
himself and had no doubt of his being able to bring the place
over to the American Interest. . . ."[18] However, Father Gibault
cautioned that ". . . his business being altogether Spiritual he
wished another person might be charged with the temporal part
of the Embassy but that he would privately direct the whole &
he named Doct' Lafont as his associate."[19] And thus the matter
was arranged.

On July 14, 1778, Dr. Jean Baptiste Laffont, Clark's official emissary to Vincennes, set out for that village, accompanied by Father Gibault, ". . . with a few others . . . ,"[20] among whom was a spy inserted into the company by Clark.[21] Besides a letter from Colonel Clark, commissioning him to undertake the enterprise, Laffont bore a proclamation to the citizens of Vincennes and several letters from private citizens of Kaskaskia to friends at Vincennes,[22] undoubtedly urging them to join the American cause. Clark's proclamation, very cleverly composed, gave the impression that he was well aware that the citizens of Vincennes, long anxious to throw off the yoke of British oppression, would joyfully embrace the blessings of liberty generously offered them by the Americans. Should they choose to take the oath of allegiance to the "Republic of Virginia," they might elect one of their number captain of a military force mustered from their citizenry, sequester the munitions in the British fort, and defend themselves ". . . until further orders. . . ."[23] No threats appeared in Clark's proclamation to the citizens of Vincennes, but in his letter to Laffont Clark warned: ". . . in case those people will not accede to offers so reasonable . . . they may expect to feel the miseries of a war. . . ."[24] In his discussions with Father Gibault, and most probably with Laffont, Clark allowed the priest to assume that a vast American force waited at the Falls of the Ohio ready, at Clark's order, to attack Vincennes. Further, Clark led Gibault, Laffont, and the citizens of Vincennes to believe that among Rocheblave's captured papers was evidence to show that the people at Vincennes were overwhelmingly in favor of the American cause. Though Clark actually procured none of Rocheblave's papers, his inference was that Vincennes had best grasp this lone opportunity to accept protection from the Americans lest the British take them for traitors. Father Gibault, too, was verbally instructed by Clark on ". . . how to act in certain cases. . . ."[25]

Setting out by horseback on July 14, 1778, Gibault and his party reached Vincennes, about 150 miles to the northeast, perhaps on July 17. After a day or two explaining the situation to the people at Vincennes, Gibault and Laffont persuaded them to forswear loyalty to the British and take the oath of allegiance to the Americans. This ceremony was performed solemnly in the church on July 20, 1778. One hundred eighty householders signed the oath or made their mark beside their names.[26] Clark reported the results of the expedition thus: "Mr. Jebault and party accompanied by several gen[tn] of St. Vincenes Returned about the first of August with the Joyfull News."[27] He promptly dispatched Captain Leonard Helm, with a few troops, to take command of the post from François Rider de Busseron whom the citizens of Vincennes had elected from their number to command the militia raised among themselves, as Clark had suggested.[28] As perhaps the Americans expected, it was not long before the British prepared to retake Vincennes as well as to march against the Illinois Country.

Informed of Clark's success at Vincennes, Henry Hamilton, lieutenant governor and commandant for the British at Detroit, procured permission to launch a campaign against that post as well as the Illinois Country. After his French troops received absolution from the venerable Jesuit missionary, Pierre Potier, Hamilton marched from Detroit, on October 7, 1778, at the head of 180 British and French militia and a contingent of Indians.[29] Seventy-one days later, on December 17, Leonard Helm, the American commander at Vincennes, whose total defensive force was less than thirty men, surrendered the place without a struggle.[30] On December 19, the harried citizens of Vincennes were again summoned to the church where they were required to ". . . declare and acknowledge . . ." that, in taking the oath of allegiance to the American cause, they had forgotten their duty to God and man.[31] "We ask pardon of God," the new oath read, "and hope for forgiveness from our legitimate sovereign, the king of England . . ." whom they hoped would forgive them and ". . . take us under his protection as good and faithful subjects, as we promise and swear to become before God and man."[32]

Not all the rebel militia at Vincennes submitted meekly to Hamilton's order. At least a few, as the British commandant reported, grasped the first opportunity to escape. Among these was:

> . . . a brother to Gibault, the priest, who had been an active Agent for the Rebels, and whose vicious and immoral conduct was sufficient to do infinite mischief in a Country where ignorance and bigotry give full scope to the depravity of a licentious ecclesiastic. This wretch it was who absolved the French inhabitants from their Allegiance to the King of Great Britain. To enumerate the Vices of the Inhabitants would be to give a long catalogue, but [to] assert that they are not in possession of a single virtue, is no more than the truth and justice require, still the most eminently vicious and scandalous was the reverend Monsieur Gibault.[33]

Hamilton's bitter denunciation of Father Gibault was not his first such remark. Before news of the fall of Vincennes reached Detroit, together with an account of Gibault's part in it, Hamilton reported, on August 8, 1778: "I have no doubt that by this time they [the Virginians] are at Vincennes, as, when the Express came away, one Gibault, a French priest, had his horse ready to go thither from Cahokia [Kaskaskia] to receive the submission of the inhabitants in the name of the Rebels."[34] It would not be difficult for Gibault to conjecture what his fate might be should he fall into Hamilton's hands. Before long that eventuality seemed to be eminently possible.

Realizing that midwinter was practically an impossible time to move against the Illinois Country, Hamilton settled down at Vincennes, spending the days preparing the fort for a possible attack from Clark's forces. During that period, which the

74

British commandant confidently expected to last until spring, various Indian tribes were contacted and scouting parties into the Illinois Country were sent out, these latter with orders to make every effort to capture Colonel Clark. In mid-January, one such small force was encountered near Kaskaskia while Clark was at Prairie du Rocher attending a ball given in his honor. When the British were discovered, they announced that they were an advanced party of a force of some 800 men who would shortly attack Kaskaskia and easily capture it. Coolly, Clark quickly returned to Kaskaskia and prepared to defend it. Father Gibault, however, could not face the possibility of the American defeat with equal equanimity since Hamilton would hardly treat him as a military prisoner of war. Of the priest's reaction, Clark reported:

> The Priest of all Men the most affraid of Mr. Hamilton, he was in the greatest consternation, determined to Act agreeble to my Instruction. I found by his Consternation that he was sure that the Fort would be taken. . . . I pretended that I wanted him to go to the Spanish side with Publick Papers and Money. the proposition pleased him well, he immediately started & getting into an Island the Ice passing so thick down the Messicippi, that he was obliged to Encamp three days in the most obscure part of the Island with only a servant to attend him.[35]

During Father Gibault's chilling exile, one poor citizen of Kaskaskia came within an ace of being hanged over the priest's situation. Clark related that while Gibault was in hiding a fresh circumstance alarmed the Cahokians.

> . . . one of the Inhabitants Riding into the Field met a Man that told him he saw a party of the Enemy going on to the Island to take the Priest, he returning to the town met the Priest's Brother in Law and told him what he had hear'd, and begged him not to tell me of it the Poor fellow half scared to death about his Brother, made all haste and told me. I took his Evidence; sent for the Citizen who could not deny it. I immediately ordered him hanged. . . . nothing would have saved his life but the appearance

of his Wife and seven small Children, which sight was too moving not to have granted them the life of their Parent on terms that put it out of his power to do any damage to me. . . .[36]

Knowing that Hamilton would certainly attack the Illinois Country as soon as weather permitted, Colonel Clark boldly determined to ". . . Risque the whole on a single Battle."[37] From François Vigo, a French trader who was present when Vincennes fell to the British, Clark ascertained that Hamilton's regulars and French volunteers hardly outnumbered his own small army. Besides, the British occupied a very badly constructed fort which they were hurrying to repair. Gambling that an attack in midwinter would come as a complete surprise, Clark determined to march immediately. On February 6, 1779, after Father Gibault delivered a ". . . very suitable discourse, and gave us absolution . . ." Clark, with 130 men, set out for Vincennes.[38] On February 24, after a march fraught with incredible difficulty, the American leader and his heroic army forced Hamilton to surrender unconditionally. The British commander with his officers was sent as a prisoner of war to Williamsburg, but the French troops accompanying the British to Vincennes were all paroled.

With this brief review of the sequence of events in mind, it is possible to approach the question of Father Gibault's participation in the American conquest of the frontier. Was Gibault an unwilling agent for George Rogers Clark or an active cooperator, gladly lending the authority of his position to the American's cause? Was he, on the contrary, neither of these, but rather a disinterested spectator, concerned only with performing his spiritual duties and, incidentally, hoping, by his presence, to avoid unnecessary bloodshed?

It may be safely presumed that Father Gibault knew Bishop Briand's unrelenting opposition to the American Revolution. On May 22, 1775, Briand published his *Mandement* addressed to ". . . all the people of this colony . . . ," condemning the

American rebels declaring that any cooperation with them was immoral and would meet with severe ecclesiastical punishment.[39] During the summer of 1775 Gibault visited Montreal, if not also Quebec, where certainly everyone, especially the clergy, was quite familiar with the bishop's published condemnation. Further, while Gibault was at Montreal, the city was threatened by an invasion from an American military force under command of General Richard Montgomery. The city fell to the Americans on November 13, 1775. After he returned to the Illinois Country, in May 1776, Father Gibault may not have learned of the grave ecclesiastical penalties leveled by Bishop Briand against clergy and laity accused of aiding the American rebels.[40] The fact remains, however, that if he even seemed cooperative toward Colonel Clark, Gibault risked seriously offending his bishop and at a time when the missionary was already under suspicion.

Gibault's attitude toward the American Revolution previous to Clark's attack on Kaskaskia cannot, apparently, be determined from any document now available. There would appear, however, little reason to suspect that he was not of the same mind as most Canadians who generally assumed that the *Bostonais* were bitterly anti-Catholic, brutally vicious and bloody warriors who traditionally hated the French. However, Colonel Clark states: "The Priest that had lately come from Canada had made himself a little acquainted with our dispute; contrary to the principal of his Brother in Canada was rather prejudiced in favor of us."[41] If Clark's judgment was correct, perhaps two factors explain Father Gibault's sympathy for the American cause. During the decade of British rule in the Illinois Country no effective local civil government emerged. Since simple public order pertained scarcely anywhere, Gibault's task as pastor constantly increased in difficulty. A second factor may have been simple propinquity. Many Americans of Anglo-Saxon ancestry migrated to the Illinois Country after 1763. There they founded businesses, intermarried with the French, and established amicable social relations with them. Pierre Gibault may well have concluded that if the British could not or would not institute civil order, the Americans might be able to do so. At very least, he may have decided that the *Bostonais* could hardly do worse than the British. The priest knew personally many Americans who certainly were not the bloodthirsty fiends common report had them to be. Perhaps these conjectures have more than a little validity for despite Clark's flamboyant description of the timorous attitude of the Kaskaskians, Gibault conducted himself with becoming dignity.

Once the people of Kaskaskia realized the small military force at Clark's command, it may be concluded with no little certainty that Father Gibault's influence played a vital part in assisting the American commander to consolidate his position. It would be unreasonable to believe that the rugged, frontier male population of Kaskaskia, outnumbering Clark's force nearly four to one, would not have driven the invading army out had not someone influenced them to the contrary. Certainly Clark played his few cards well. Informing the people that he represented a force which had just concluded an alliance with the king of France weighed heavily in his favor when the people discussed their situation among themselves. Also, the American leader's apparent respect for religion, manifested almost immediately after his arrival, must have rendered his presence at least less obnoxious to those of the citizens who felt that the invaders must surely be devils incarnate. Nonetheless, the delicate situation required, on the part of the Kaskaskians, a leader whom all respected in order to mediate effectively with the invaders. And that leader, as Clark himself attested, was Father Pierre Gibault.

The consummate prudence with which Kaskaskia's pastor approached Colonel Clark the morning after the town fell into his hands speaks well for the missionary. Once the townspeople

were disarmed, no trouble could possibly arise if the people re-
sumed normal activities. Would Colonel Clark, therefore, ". . .
give" the priest "liberty to perform his duties in his church
. . . ?"[42] Or, as Clark put it in a later memoir: ". . . the priest
informed me . . . that as the Inhabitants expected to be separated never perhaps to meet again they begged through him that
they might be permitted to spend some time in the church to
take their leave of each other. . . ."[43] Whichever of Clark's accounts be the more accurate, Father Gibault showed himself the
prudent diplomat, even though Clark deliberately sought to discourage him ". . . from pe[ti]tioning again. . . ."[44]

Requesting the minimum, Father Gibault arranged for both
religious services and an opportunity for the people to discuss
their prospects, determining how best to take advantage of them.
Reaching the decision to save what they could, Gibault, with
the principal citizens of the village, was delegated to return to
Colonel Clark to thank him for his consideration. Granted a second audience, the delegation, through Gibault, their spokesman,
again sought only the minimum consideration. If the people
were now to be driven from their homes, would the colonel permit families to remain together, taking with them sufficient provisions to ward off starvation and give them a new start wherever
they might be sent?[45] In these new negotiations, Father Gibault
acted the proper role of pastor, protecting his flock from spiritual and material disaster. But also, he quite evidently thereby
won the respect of Colonel Clark, a difficult and, by his own ad-
mission, a highly irascible man. Thenceforth, Clark consulted
Gibault regarding his subsequent plans.

In preparing for the conquest of Vincennes, it is not precisely clear, from Clark's reports, specifically who suggested the
method of attack successfully employed. In his report to George
Mason, November 19, 1779, Clark credited Gibault with sug-
gesting the method of gaining control of Vincennes. "Post S$^t$
Vincent," he related, "a Town about the Size of Williamsburg

was the next Object in my view. . . . M^r Jeboth, the Priest, to fully convince me of his Attachment offered to undertake to win that Town for me if I would permit him and let a few of them go; . . . the Priest told me he would go himself, and gave me to understand, that although he had nothing to do with temporal business, that he would give them such hints in a spiritual way that would be very conducive to the business. . . ."[46] Strengthening this testimony is Clark's statement regarding Gibault in the colonel's instructions to Jean Baptiste Laffont, who, at the priest's suggestion, was Clark's official ambassador to the citizens of Vincennes. Laffont was specifically instructed: "You are to act in concert with M. le Curé, who, I hope, will prepare the citizens to grant your demands."[47]

Clark's testimony concerning Gibault's part in the winning of Vincennes merits critical examination. From the outset, the missionary quite properly insisted that as the representative of the Prince of Peace he could have no part in encouraging armed conflict. He was willing, however, to employ his influence at Vincennes, urging everyone to avoid bloodshed, which, in effect, amounted to encouraging the people to follow the example of their friends at Kaskaskia. He did, however, accept responsibility for keep a journal of events connected with the expedition to Vincennes, a document which has, unfortunately, not survived.[48] It would be unrealistic to ignore the fact that Father Gibault's very presence with the Laffont delegation influenced the townspeople at Vincennes in favor of the proposition offered by their visitors. Gibault was certainly the best known of those arriving as quite obviously the most respected.

At Father Gibault's request, Jean Baptiste Laffont, official leader of the expedition to Vincennes, wrote a letter to Clark, on August 7, 1778, explaining the priest's part in the expedition:

> I cannot but approve of what M. Gibault said in his journal. If he omitted some historical facts which might have been worthy of inclusion, what he said is the simple truth. All that he asked

me to add, which he will tell you in my presence, at his request, and which he forgot, is that in all civil matters, not only with the French but with the Indians, he meddled with nothing, because he was not ordered to do so and it was opposed to his exhortation tending towards peace and union and the prevention of bloodshed. And so, sir, as for the temporal affairs with which I am wholly entrusted, I hope to have [given] complete satisfaction for I acted in all things with irreproachable integrity.[49]

Years later, Father Gibault cited Laffont's letter as incontrovertible proof that he, personally, did not exceed the bounds of his sacerdotal office.

Documentation from Father Gibault's own hand concerning his part in the submission of Vincennes is confined to a very few letters. On April 1, 1783, the missionary wrote to his bishop: "I hope to send your Lordship . . . a detailed account of everything that has happened here during the past four or five years."[50] At sometime previous to 1788 Gibault fulfilled his promise, but that letter has not survived.[51] The first extant document from Gibault's own hand referring to the submission of Vincennes occurs in a letter to Bishop Briand written at Vincennes on June 6, 1786, almost a decade after the event:

As for the people at Post Vincennes, whom, it is said in Canada, I led to perjury, perhaps the people themselves, to avoid trouble with Governor Henry Hamilton, laid all the blame on me. Or perhaps Hamilton himself and his officers used the pretext that such uninformed people would not have allowed themselves to be persuaded except by me. On that supposition the people were pardoned for their defection, laying the whole blame on me. The truth is that not having visited Post Vincennes for a long time and finding a favorable occasion for going there with Mr. Laffont, who was well attended, I profited by the occasion to tend to my mission. If I had meddled in a matter of such importance my signature would have appeared somewhere. Other proofs would have been offered than those of "they say," "we heard it reported," and other similar accusations. On account of certain complaints about me on that subject, I had the good fortune to obtain from Mr. Laffont himself a declaration on the subject as soon as we returned to Illinois. I am sending you the original of that certificate, written by his own hand, keeping for myself only a copy, lest I be rendered suspect. You may judge more certainly from a document than from mere idle words.[52]

Gibault's final extant word to his bishop on the Vincennes incident is contained in his letter of May 22, 1788, in which he pleaded to be recalled to Canada. After adducing reasons of health and his repugnance to serve under a Spanish or an American bishop, the wearied missionary campaigner added:

> As for opposition to me because of the fear that I was or may have been active for the American republic, you have only to re-read my first letter in which I gave you an account of our capture, and my last letter in which I sent you a certificate attesting to my conduct at Post Vincennes, in the capture of which they say I had taken a hand. You will see that not only did I not meddle in anything, but on the contrary I have always regretted and still do regret every day the loss of the mildness of British rule.[53]

Father Gibault's many subsequent denials of complicity with the Americans are not readily reconciled with his actions. Of no small import was his position regarding the people forswearing loyalty to George III and taking an oath of allegiance to the state of Virginia. At Kaskaskia, the morality of advising the people to change their loyalty presented no problem. Kaskaskia fell to an invading army which had a clear right to require from the people a change of allegiance or emigration. As pastor, Gibault could in good conscience advise his flock to accept one or other alternative. The situation was quite otherwise at Vincennes. There, the people, proselytized by their friends, were not conquered by an army. Father Gibault must have been consulted regarding the morality of changing allegiance. This is, perhaps, the meaning of Clark's remark that Gibault offered to give the people at Vincennes ". . . such hints in a spiritual way that would be very conducive to the business. . . ."[54] The spiritual advice could properly pertain to the moral propriety of forswearing loyalty to the English. Confirmatory of the conclusion that Gibault was intimately associated with the oath taken at Vincennes is the very fact that the ceremony took place in the church. It is highly unlikely that such an important event would have occurred in that particular place without the pastor's consent. Further, given the season, late July, there was no reason for not holding a meeting at the fort or in the open if the pastor found himself morally unable to subscribe to the ceremony. Nor may it be argued that since Gibault's name does not appear on the document signed by those taking the oath that he had no part in it. The reasonable presumption is that Gibault had already sworn allegiance to the American cause at Kaskaskia. If he had not, Clark would hardly have allowed the priest to join the delegation to Vincennes, no matter in what capacity.

Pierre Gibault could not properly protest, as he later did to his bishop, that he was in no sense an official of Clark's delegation to Vincennes. Besides dealing with the French there, the priest, at Clark's request, contacted Tobacco's Son, chief of the Piankashaw band of the Miami, conveying to the Indian Clark's compliments, that is, offering the chief the friendship of the American invader.[55] Thereafter, the Miami remained allies of the Americans, or at least held themselves neutral.

A point equally demonstrative of Gibault's official capacity at Vincennes is that Colonel Clark submitted to the Virginia legislature a bill for the priest's expenses. Among the items listed in Clark's inventory of expenses for his western expedition is found: "M. Gibault . . . expenses in taking possession of Post Vincennes in 1779, $657.00."[56] We know also that Clark furnished the horse Gibault used on the expedition.[57] Perhaps no less confirmatory of his official character at Vincennes was Gibault's memorial to Congress, requesting a grant of land on the basis of his services there ". . . which are not unknown to you. . . ."[58]

Since these facts are obviously incontrovertible, how does one explain Father Gibault's protestations to his bishop that he went to Vincennes with Laffont only because the expeditionary party offered him an opportunity to travel there safely in order to perform his normal spiritual functions? Certainly Gibault did say Mass and confer the sacraments during his brief stay. Since his last visit to Vincennes, June 1771, forty-one infants had been privately baptized. For all of these the priest supplied the solemn ceremonies which a layman may not perform. He also baptized an Indian slave and witnessed four marriages.[59] If the missionary had limited himself to these spiritual duties, he could, perhaps, be absolved of any collaboration in the civic purpose of the expedition. However, such was far from the case.

Perhaps the only satisfactory answer to the dilemma lies in attempting to understand Father Gibault's volatile character which inclined him to extremes of enthusiasm and discouragement. For example, as has been indicated, when he first came to Kaskaskia he was lavish in his praise of the people. Within five years he was bitterly condemnatory of them. What Gibault's attitude may actually have been contemporary to the events is now unavailable from any documentary source thus far discovered. Remaining documentation from his own hand manifests a certain disillusionment. Gibault's clearest declaration in his own defense, his letter to Briand written a decade after the incidents, is, perhaps, basically a rather bitter denunciation of local administration by the Americans. They did not establish solid civil order in the Illinois Country nor did the French there fare well at the hands of the American officials. Besides, ecclesiastical jurisdiction over the Illinois Country was in a state of flux. Given his temperament, it is not impossible that Gibault rationalized his later position. By that time he may well have become convinced that he really did not aid Colonel Clark or that he had any official hand in causing the British to lose Vincennes.

Whatever Pierre Gibault's opinion may have been, the Americans were quite ready to give him credit for the success of the operation at Vincennes. Informed of the priest's part in the matter, Governor Patrick Henry, on December 15, 1778, directed Colonel Clark: "I beg you will please present my Compliments to Mr. Gibault and Doctor Lafong & thank them for me for their good services to the state."[60] Three days previously the governor wrote to Clark: "Upon a fair presumption that the people about Detroit have Similar Inclinations with those at Illinois and Wabash, I think it possible that they may be brought to expel their British Masters & become fellow Citizens of a free state. I recommend this to your Serious Consideration, and to consult with some confidential persons on the subject. Perhaps Mr. Gibault the Priest (to whom this Country owes many thanks for his Zeal and Services) may promote this affair."[61]

It would appear justified, then, to maintain that Father Gibault at least suggested to Clark the strategy whereby Vincennes was induced to surrender peacefully. Though the missionary may not have subscribed, wholeheartedly, to the principles which the American cause represented, he willingly cooperated with Clark if only to avoid bloodshed. By thus assisting the Americans, Gibault laid himself open to sharp criticism from his bishop and rendered himself so suspect to the British that his homeland was forever closed to him. As for the Americans, little appreciation was subsequently manifested by them for Pierre Gibault who, after all, was, in no small measure, responsible for George Rogers Clark's success.

---

## THE FLUCTUATING

## AMERICAN FRONTIER

After cooperating so generously with George Rogers Clark in wresting the Illinois Country from British control, the fondest hopes of the French must have been for a rapid revival of stable civil government as well as the prompt development of a solid economy. The people surely were delighted with Clark's immediate establishment of civil courts, even though they probably understood that these would eventually give way to other and more permanent institutions under the commonwealth of Virginia. In his memoir, Clark reported:

> I inquired particularly into the manner the people had been Governed formerly and much to my satisfaction [found] that it

had Gen^ly [been] as sevear as under the Military Law. I was determined to make an advantage of it and took every step in my power to cause the people to feell the blessings Injoyed by an American Citizen which I soon discovered inabled me to support [obtain?] from their own choice almost a supream authority over them. I caused a Court of sivil Judicature to be Established at Kohas [Cahokia] Elected by the people. Maj^r Bowman to the supprise of the people held a pole for a Majestacy and was elected and acted as Judge of the Court. The policy of M^r Bowman holding a pole is easily perseived. After this similar Courts ware in the Towns of Kaskas [Kaskaskia] and S^t Vincenes. No people ever had their business done more to their satisfaction that [than?] they had through the means of this Regulation for a considerable time.[1]

Colonel Clark's judiciary arrangements for the Illinois Country shortly gave way to more permanent governmental trappings. As soon as the necessity was realized, the Virginia legislature passed an act, on December 9, 1778, establishing the county of Illinois.[2] By it, all who took an oath of fidelity to the commonwealth of Virginia enjoyed all the rights of citizens, including freedom of religion, ". . . which the inhabitants shall fully, and to all intents and purposes enjoy, together with all their civil rights and property."[3] The chief executive of Virginia's new territory was a county lieutenant, appointed by the governor, who also held office as chief military commander. All civil officials ". . . to which the . . . inhabitants have been accustomed . . ." were to be elected by a majority of the people.[4] These officials were directed to exercise jurisdiction ". . . agreeable to the laws which the present settlers are now accustomed to."[5] Thus, until such time as the new citizens residing in the county of Illinois accustomed themselves to the laws of Virginia, they would continue civil life within the legal framework with which they were familiar, even including the same customary legal officials such as notaries and the like. One can properly surmise that the French were exceedingly pleased when the details of Virginia's act were made known to them. However, as is always the case in all human activity, theory and practice are not quite the same.

The new civil government was inaugurated by John Todd, the first to hold office as county lieutenant, at Kaskaskia on May 12, 1779.[6] On that day, Colonel Clark, assembling the citizens before the church door, presented Todd as ". . . the only person in the state [of Virginia] whom I desired to fill this post. . . ."[7] Todd, in his turn, assured the gathering that the "Republic of Virginia" had come to the Illinois Country ". . . not for love of conquest, but to invite you to enjoy with her the blessings of independence, free and equal, and to be judged and governed by officers who will be placed in power by the people."[8] Thereupon, those eligible elected ". . . six of the most judicious men to act as judges of the court. . . ."[9] The whole of the county of Illinois was divided into three districts, Kaskaskia, Cahokia, and Vincennes, each with its quota of judges, including representatives from the smaller villages within the individual districts.[10]

The establishment of a new civil government failed to effect the Utopia the people expected. One of their pressing problems was the chaotic state of money. All of those able to do so had contributed funds or supplies to Colonel Clark who had issued, in payment, paper money of the Continental Congress or drafts drawn on the supposed credit of the commonwealth of Virginia. When those holding the notes attempted to collect they sorrowfully discovered that the paper was practically worthless since both the Continental Congress and Virginia were bankrupt.[11] In an effort to bring about some financial stability, Todd recalled all paper money, promising that eventually both the Congress and Virginia would redeem their notes.[12] Barely $20,000 was surrendered, but even that small amount was never redeemed.[13]

The financial crisis was all the more disastrous simply because of the people's new allegiance to the Americans. The traditional economic market for the area's produce, chiefly peltries and wheat, was Montreal. But by Clark's conquest of the country, Canada, as a market, was closed to the merchants and farmers of the Mississippi Valley. Even if that had not been true, the trade route to the St. Lawrence River valley was highly unsafe since the British were known to be mounting an attack against the Americans to regain their lost territory. In any case, there was little to market for the war left small opportunity for gathering peltries and persistent droughts had ruined the crops.

If all of these misfortunes were not discouraging enough, once the actual campaigning ended Clark's soldiers, garrisoned in the various villages, manifested all the worst characteristics of armies of occupation. What military commanders did not arbitrarily requisition, the troops, on their own, "liberated" with the utmost impunity. For example, only a month after John Todd took office, the newly elected magistrates at Kaskaskia presented him with a memorial complaining that the soldiers had driven domestic animals off the village common and taken them to the fort where the beasts were slaughtered. The memorial said, in part: "They [the soldiers] announce to us that this is a free country, where each one should be master to do with his property, as pleases him and to enjoy it, as he may see fit, yet they have killed plow-oxen, milch cows and other animals, which belonged to persons and people who could not get along without them, being for some, needful for the cultivation of the land, and to others for the subsistence and nourishment of their families."[14]

It was not long before military commanders were requisitioning flour and other staple necessities without regard for the dire poverty of most of the people. The situation became so desperate that, on November 18, 1780, the Kaskaskians registered a complaint with Colonel John Rogers, commanding the troops, stating that they simply could not furnish the supplies demanded. "Consider then," they wrote, "our situation and see how impossible it is for us to give you the subsistence, since we do not have it ourselves. You must know, moreover, that the intention of the government is not to ruin us, and that Colonel Clark gave us the choice of keeping or not keeping the troops here. . . . In short, . . . the inhabitants in general have the honor to declare to you that they are unable, on account of their poverty, of which you surely are not ignorant, to make any provision for you."[15]

If all of these difficulties were not sufficient to discourage the French, they were also plagued with an influx of Yankees, speculators, drifters, sharp merchants, and the like, whose outlook and attitudes, not to say values, were at variance with the original inhabitants. The frontier American was a loner, given to making his way by the strength of his good right arm. He settled his differences in brawling, gouging, and generally acting the part of a roistering troublemaker. Law to him resided really in the strength of his two fists. He did not look to the courts to settle any difference arising between him and another; rather he simply challenged his opponent in physical combat. If he was defeated, he retreated with what chastened pride he could muster, satisfied or not. In contrast, the French were by tradition and training a very orderly folk who looked to the courts to settle their differences. For which reason the two peoples tended to stand off from one another, to foster mutual distrust and to avoid mingling. It was many years before that simple sociological problem would find solution. In the meantime, the less attractive features of each group remained all too evident.

Unhappily, conditions in the villages of the Illinois Country progressed from bad to worse. A little over six months after assuming office, John Todd departed for the East, leaving his deputy, Richard Winston, in charge.[16] In his turn, Winston succeeded hardly any better than his predecessor, perhaps because not even Virginia took an active interest in its valuable new county. When the one year for which the Virginia legislature had approved the act establishing the county ended, the vital instrument was renewed for a second year. But at the end of that period the act was allowed to lapse.[17] Winston departed in 1783, turning over his, by then, questionable authority to Timothé Boucher de Montbrun.[18] The Virginia legislature made one final effort to adjust the tangled affairs of the county of Illinois by appointing a commission, in 1782, to examine the situation at close hand. The commissioners convened at the Falls of the Ohio on January 15, 1782, but no one appeared to file a complaint.[19]

Thereafter practical anarchy reigned in the Illinois Country until 1790. This sorry state of affairs was thus described by François Carbonneaux, clerk of the practically inoperative court at Kaskaskia: "The greatest disorder prevailed. The most flagrant crimes were committed with impunity. A man might be murdered in his house and the crime go unpunished since the settlements possessed neither sheriffs nor prisons."[20] And Pierre Gibault was left, almost single-handed, to strive morally against that new Babylon.

Though Father Gibault had his hands full attempting to encourage the practice of religion among a nearly rebellious flock, probably unknown to him a major crisis was developing between himself and his major ecclesiastical superior, the bishop of Quebec. In 1777, as was noted above, Bishop Briand informed Gibault that an ecclesiastical investigator was being dispatched to examine into the spiritual and, perhaps, financial state of Gibault's mission as well as the irregularities and supposedly unclerical conduct of Gibault himself. The appointed visitor, Father Jean-François Hubert, certainly obtained a passport, on August 21, 1778, at Montreal to visit the Illinois Country, but whether he ever actually reached Kaskaskia or any other village within Gibault's mission cannot be incontrovertibly demonstrated from any known contemporary document still extant.[21]

If Father Hubert left Montreal shortly after August 21, 1778, he would have reached Detroit at least by early September. At that post, the commandant, Henry Hamilton, was preparing to attack the Illinois Country, having learned on August 6, 1778, that George Rogers Clark had conquered it.[22] Under the circumstances, it would seem surprising if Hamilton had allowed Father Hubert to proceed, unescorted, to the Illinois Country, since the priest would inevitably fall into Clark's hands and be able to inform the American of Hamilton's military strength. It is more reasonable, in the absence of any positive evidence to the contrary, to conclude that Hubert advanced no farther than Detroit, returning to Quebec in the spring of 1779.[23]

What, then, explains the following formal letter from Bishop Briand to Gibault, a document by which the bishop officially suspended the missionary from exercising any ecclesiastical functions until he had presented himself to his ecclesiastical superior?

Jean-Olivier Briand, by the grace of God and the appointment of the Holy See, Bishop of Quebec, to Pierre Gibault, priest of our diocese of Quebec: Be it known to you by these presents that we have revoked and do revoke all, whatsoever, faculties and licenses previously granted you by our letter given at Quebec on May 3, 1768, attested by our signature and seal and countersigned by our secretary, Hubert. By these presents we forbid you to exercise, under any circumstances, the aforementioned faculties, licenses or powers granted in the letter previously noted. Nor may you dare in any way or under any pretext exercise these powers, whether pertaining to the office and dignity of vicar general, special or universal, or whether to the office of pastor or simple priest (excepting, however, the celebration of Mass). Wherefore, you are forbidden under pain of suspension to hear the confessions of the faithful, to preach the word of God, or to confer the sacraments or [perform] any other ecclesiastical function, and this throughout the whole of our diocese, until you have presented yourself to us. Wherefore, we command you, under pain of the same suspension, that, promptly on learning our will in your regard, by virtue of the prohibition and command issued in these presents, you immediately depart from your mission and come to us without any delay. If, however, it is impossible for you to make the journey, you are to send us, immediately, a report concerning the state of your missions and the condition of the people dwelling in those regions. If circumstances or whatever [other] cause oblige you to delay the journey, be it known to you that you may not, licitly and validly, exercise any function, either that of vicar general or of a priest, except the celebration of Mass.

Given at Quebec under our signature and seal and countersigned by our secretary.

June 12, 1780.                                        ✠ J. O. Bishop of Quebec.[24]

Historians commenting on the above letter generally accept the explanation offered for it by Auguste Gosselin who declares that Hubert, reaching the Illinois Country in the fall of 1778, ". . . returned the following year and it is believed that the news he bore concerning . . . the unfortunate Gibault obliged the pious prelate to issue an interdict."[25] Gosselin adds that ". . . Gibault, hastening to Quebec, fell at the feet of his bishop, whom he was seeing for the last time, and arose forgiven."[26] However, that highly respected author offers no documentary evidence either for Hubert's supposed presence in the Illinois Country, or his report to Briand, nor yet for Gibault's presumed visit to Quebec sometime during or shortly after June 1780.

Peculiarly, those who have written about this rather mysterious incident concerning Gibault are generally guilty of a strange error which they should have avoided since most of them were themselves ecclesiastics who certainly were well aware of the technical meaning of the canonical term *interdict*. Ecclesiastically, interdict is defined as a censure, or penalty, imposed by the Church on a group of Catholics, such as a nation, a city, or perhaps a parish. It is canonically possible for the proper ecclesiastical authority to impose an interdict on an individual cleric, but, if done, the cleric, of whatever rank, is, by reason of that penalty, forbidden to celebrate Mass, if he is a priest. And, it will have been noticed, that Briand specifically stated that Father Gibault was permitted to continue doing this. Suspension,

93

however, is a penalty whereby a cleric is excluded from an ecclesiastical office he holds and/or from receiving whatever benefits arise from the office.[27] In his letter to Gibault, both in the Latin and the French versions, Bishop Briand specifically named the censure imposed a suspension.

It has been suggested that Bishop Briand's action against Gibault was motivated by the latter's irresponsibility in disposing of property at Cahokia owned by the members of the Missions-Etrangères at Quebec. This surmise is possibly based on a petition of the inhabitants of Cahokia submitted to the American Congress on July 15, 1786, protesting sale of land surrounding their village which had been granted to the Missions-Etrangères by the king of France. Speaking of Gibault's part in disposing of the land, the people declared: ". . . M. Gibault, a priest, . . . has dared to arrogate secretly the power of disposing of this prairie by conceding it to Colonel Clark, who has resold this same concession to M. Pentecoste. . . . It has never been in the power of any ecclesiastic of the Illinois Country to dispose of the property of the subjects."[28] The assertion was completely inaccurate first because the inhabitants of Cahokia had no legal claim to the land and, secondly, because the legal owners, the Missions-Etrangères had, in 1768, given Gibault power of attorney to act for them in the Illinois Country.[29] Over the years, Gibault may have disposed of various parcels of the property, forwarding the funds obtained to the original owners at Quebec. One such transaction is recorded in the following document:

> I, the undersigned priest, vicar general of His Lordship, the Bishop of Quebec, fiscal procurator of the seigneurs of Kaokias [Cahokia], do hereby certify to have conceded and do hereby concede a town lot of one hundred and fifty feet in front by one hundred and fifty feet in width, bounded on one side by the street, on two others by the Domaine, on the fourth side by Jacques Lagrange, to Joseph Poirier, to have and to hold the same in full

propriety, but, however, subject to acknowledgement. In testimony whereof, I have signed at Kaokias this fifteenth day of May, 1778.
P. Gibault, Priest, Vicar General.[30]

The document was forwarded to the administrative officials of the Missions-Etrangères at Quebec who sent back approval:

We, the directors, superior and procurator of the Quebec Seminary, do hereby ratify and confirm, inasmuch as the same may be required, the concession hereinabove made by M. Gibault, subject to the condition that the possessor shall pay to the original owners of the soil, by way of acknowledgement, the ground rent that shall be determined by the authorities of the place. Quebec, 16th August, 1784.
Bedard, Priest, of the Seminary
Gravé, Priest, Procurator of the Seminary.[31]

Being in constant, intimate contact with the priests at his seminary, Bishop Briand could hardly have been unaware that the Missions-Etrangères had appointed Father Gibault their representative in the Illinois Country on the occasion of his departure in 1768. This is all the more certain since it was Father Hubert, for years the bishop's secretary, who signed the original document granting Gibault power of attorney. Further, in 1786, when the Cahokians denied that Father Gibault was empowered to dispose of land, the directors of the Missions-Etrangères forwarded a certified copy of the original document.[32]

The most obvious explanation for Briand's imposing the severe ecclesiastical penalty of suspension on Pierre Gibault lies in the bishop's unswerving determination to make certain that the clergy and the Catholic people in his diocese remained clearly and steadfastly loyal to the king of England. Since the British conquest of New France in 1760, no effort had been made by that officially Protestant government to inhibit the practice of the Catholic religion in Canada, though in England itself Catholicism was outlawed. Quite possibly Briand sincerely believed that if many of the clergy or even large numbers of the

Catholic people favored the Americans in their struggle for independence, the British would retaliate by suppressing Catholicity in Canada. This would seem to have been the underlying motive for the suspension imposed on Father Pierre Floquet at Montreal in June 1776.[33]

After occupying Montreal, on November 13, 1775, the Americans, commanded by General Richard Montgomery, succeeded in enlisting two companies of native Canadians, despite Bishop Briand's severe prohibition, forbidding Catholics from collaborating with the invaders.[34] Father Floquet, missionary to the Indians in the neighborhood of Montreal, manifested a certain sympathy toward the Americans whose commander had returned to the priest's use the mission rectory which had been previously commandeered as a barrack by the British. At Easter, 1776, when the Canadians serving in the American army wished to go to confession and receive Holy Communion, Floquet cared for them in spite of the bishop's prohibition. However, Father Floquet required the men to swear that they would not participate in any hostile campaign against their fellow countrymen. At about the same time, April 1776, an American commission, including Father John Carroll, future bishop of Baltimore, and his cousin, Charles Carroll of Carrollton, came to Montreal, hoping to induce the Canadians to join the American cause. Since both Fathers Carroll and Floquet had been members of the recently suppressed Society of Jesus, Carroll called on Floquet, but he neither stayed with him nor did he function as a priest at the mission chapel. Shortly before June 17, 1776, Father Etienne Mongolfier, Briand's vicar-general at Montreal, reported Floquet's "scandalous" conduct to the bishop who, thereupon, suspended the sixty-year-old missionary.[35] The suspension was not revoked until November 1776 after Floquet submitted an abject letter of apology, saying: "I humbly supplicate Your Lordship to pardon me and remove the interdict which my misdoings have drawn."[36] Bishop Briand was in no mood to look kindly on any deviation from his expressed position.

Bishop Briand would certainly have imposed ecclesiastical suspension on Father Gibault if he had been aware of the missionary's association with George Rogers Clark, especially considering the priest's part in the capture of Vincennes. But, was the bishop aware of this and, if so, how could he have come to possess the information? In reporting his activities between 1776 and 1781, Henry Hamilton, British lieutenant governor at Detroit, recorded that, encouraged by Lord George Germaine to induce the Indians to harass the western frontiers of Virginia and Pennsylvania, he dispatched several such bands with orders to refrain from their usual barbarities and to bring back as many prisoners as possible.[37] By September 15, 1778, when Hamilton marched from Detroit to attack Vincennes, the Indians had brought him 129 ". . . prisoners of different ages and sexes. . . ."[38] By that date, Father Hubert certainly would have reached Detroit. Also, Hamilton had known since August 6 that Vincennes was in American hands. Only a week after the British forces set out from Detroit for Vincennes, Hamilton wrote to his commander, General Frederick Haldimand, ". . . Gibault the Priest has been active for the Rebels. I shall try to award him if possible."[39] Since Hamilton can be presumed to have possessed information about Gibault before he left Detroit, if Father Hubert was there he certainly could have informed Briand that Gibault was at least suspected of disloyalty to the British.

More detailed information concerning Father Gibault's relationship to the Americans was probably gathered from another source. It will be remembered that the British wrested Vincennes from American control on December 17, 1778. From that date until February 24, 1779, Hamilton's eighty soldiers lived at the fort and quite certainly mingled with the townsfolk who must have related the details of their surrender to the Americans. Undoubtedly, Father Gibault's part in the capture was recalled, over and over, especially to the French-speaking soldiers under Hamilton's command. When Clark defeated Hamilton at Vincennes, he held as prisoners of war only Hamilton and twenty-five soldiers. He allowed the others to return home, provided they swore not to bear arms against the Americans for the duration of the war.[40] Many of these men returned to Detroit where they certainly must have elaborated on the details of their venture, probably including what they knew of Gibault's activity concerning Vincennes. This information could quite readily have been forwarded to Quebec since that line of communication was not closed by the war.

In the eyes of their Indian allies, the British prestige declined alarmingly because of their humiliating defeat at Vincennes. Hence, it became vital for the English to erase that disaster by a clear and crushing defeat of the Americans. Therefore, orders were issued to gather a sufficiently large force of troops and Indian allies to march successfully against Clark.[41] This army was directed to gather at Michilimackinac under command of Patrick Sinclair, lieutenant governor stationed at that fort. Reporting progress, Sinclair wrote to General Haldimand's aide-de-camp, D. Brehm, on October 15, 1779:

> General Carleton and the Bishop sent up one Gibon [Gibault] a priest on a mission for reasons best known to themselves, the part which he has represented in the Rebel interest, and may hereafter improve upon, requires in my humble opinion a mandate from Mon Seigneur for his appearance at Quebec. His conduct will certainly justify me to the General in making this representation, and I do it to avoid any future severity which may, by means of the Indians, be necessary to direct against an individual of the sacred and respected clergy.[42]

When neither Carleton nor Briand took speedy action, Sinclair again brought up Gibault's case in a letter to Brehm. After discussing some details regarding the church and the pastor's residence at Michilimackinac, Sinclair continued:

98

The subject leads me to inquire whether or not Monseignur Bri-
and will issue out two mandates for the appearance of the Vaga-
bond Gibault who stiles himself the Vicar General of the Illinois.
Allow me in an official capacity to request that you will mention
this again to the General as indispensably necessary. Let them be
sent to me. I will forward them and publish them at the Illinois
in order to blast any remains of reputation which the wretch may
have been able to preserve among Scoundrels almost as worthless
as himself.[43]

On April 17, 1780, Brehm replied to Sinclair: "His Excellency
will likewise profit of your Information of Pere Gibeau."[44]

After these communications, the bishop certainly must have
been only too painfully aware that Father Gibault was officially
considered a traitor by the British authorities. A little less than
two months after the date of Brehm's letter to Sinclair, Bishop
Briand issued his letter suspending Father Gibault, on June 12,
1780. The document was sent by way of Detroit, as is noted on
Briand's copy of the letter now preserved in the archives of the
Archdiocese of Quebec.

Whether Pierre Gibault ever received his bishop's letter
suspending him will, perhaps, always remain a mystery. Certainly the missionary continued his regular ecclesiastical duties
without a sufficiently lengthy interruption to have permitted him
to complete the tiring round-trip journey to Quebec. There is no
extant letter from Gibault to Briand during the period. The first
letter from Gibault to his bishop after the American invasion of
the Illinois Country is a very brief note, dated April 1, 1783,
from Ste. Genevieve. This contains no reference to the matter of
suspension. Nor is there any reference to a suspension in any
subsequent letter written to his bishop by the missionary. There
is an oblique reference to the matter, a remark found in the
memorial of the inhabitants of Cahokia to the American Congress. They declared that when Father Gibault negotiated the
sale of the land about which they were complaining that ". . .
he was under interdict by order of the bishop of Canada, and we

do not know if that interdict is yet removed; but all interdicts annul all acts and contracts which the one so interdicted may have made while it lasted."[45]

The people of Cahokia were in error regarding both the chronology and the canonical effects of an interdict, or properly in Gibault's case, a suspension. The land transaction, about which the Cahokians were complaining, occurred on May 7, 1779, over a full year before Bishop Briand issued his letter suspending Gibault.[46] Suspensions and interdicts deprive clerics of ecclesiastical privileges, not civil rights. In acting as the agent of the Missions-Etrangères in the Illinois Country, Gibault was performing a purely secular service wholly unrelated to any ecclesiastical function or jurisdiction.

While Bishop Briand was issuing his declaration of suspension to Pierre Gibault, the missionary, apparently completely ignorant of the fact, was wholly occupied with attempting to bring about a return to normal religious life in the Mississippi Valley after its capture by the Americans. While Clark was off building a fort on the Ohio River, Gibault wrote him on May 10, 1780: "We are very poor and destitute of all things. . . . We fear the savages and the evilly disposed people who are urging them to kill us. In a word we are truly in a sad situation."[47]

Despite physical dangers and the much more discouraging indifference of his people, Gibault faithfully continued to minister to the villages of Prairie du Rocher and Kaskaskia. He seemed to have been relieved of the responsibility of serving Cahokia which was cared for by Father Bernard de Limpach, a German by birth, who came to New Orleans in 1772 and was appointed pastor of St. Louis on February 18, 1776.[48] Sometime during 1780, or shortly thereafter, Gibault took up permanent residence at Ste. Geneviève where he remained until approximately 1785. While no documentary evidence survives satisfactorily explaining this extraordinary move, the possible reason lies in the notoriously contentious character of the Kaskaskians.

Confirmatory of that conclusion is a letter from Lieutenant John Rice Jones to Major Hamtramck. Jones writes concerning a complaint about the people of Kaskaskia submitted to him by a Father Le Dru who served briefly as pastor of Kaskaskia: "He met with no better usage than . . . Mr. Gibault before him did; and I am well persuaded that any other priest will not find a better reception until the establishment of a government."[49] A specific instance of the sort of problem arising for Father Gibault at Kaskaskia bears quoting:

> At court, February 7, 1782
> G. Blin shows the Court that the named Pierre Lafleur had had a high mass sung by M. Gibault and that he had asked the latter several times to pay the *fabrique* which the latter refused to do. Therefore he prays that some of his moveables, up to the equivalent of what he owes be attached. The court ordered that the named Pierre Lafleur be summoned to the next Court to answer the complaint brought against him.
> The Court adjourned to March 7, 1782.              Present:
> President G. Blin                    Jos. Cesirre
>            P. Grandmont              Bte. Saucier
>            J. Bte. Lacroix           Bte. Dubuque[50]

Ste. Genevieve, it will be recalled, came into the possession of the crown of Spain by virtue of the secret Treaty of San Ildefonso, November 3, 1762, whereby France ceded to Spain all her territory west of the Mississippi River. In due time ecclesiastical jurisdiction over Spain's new area came under the responsibility of the see of Santiago de Cuba.[51] The bishop of that diocese, Jaime José de Echeverria, appointed a Spanish Capuchin, Father Cyrillo de Barcelona, his representative at New Orleans.[52] Thus, for Father Gibault, moving his residence to Ste. Genevieve meant, as he well knew, placing himself under the jurisdiction of Father Cyrillo. In a quite true sense, if the move were to be permanent, Gibault perforce divorced himself from any legal attachment to the bishop of Quebec. The prospect of such a drastic change must have greatly concerned Gibault, but he promptly recognized the jurisdictional change by noting in parish records that he exercised ecclesiastical authority through delegation granted him from New Orleans. For instance, in recording a marriage, the missionary noted that he was serving the parish at Ste. Genevieve by reason of authority granted by ". . . the Reverend Father Cyrillo, Vicar of Louisiana."[53]

According to their new Spanish masters, the people of Ste. Genevieve, some 400 whites and 300 slaves in 1773,[54] enjoyed no better a reputation than their neighbors at Kaskaskia across the river. Don Pedro Piernas, first Spanish governor of the Illinois territory, reported to his superior, Alejandro O'Reilly, governor of the Spanish province of Louisiana:

> License, laxity of conduct, and vice are the characteristics of its [the area's] inhabitants. Religion is given but scant respect, or to speak more correctly, is totally neglected, whether because of the abandonment of the obligations which distinguish a Catholic from a gentile given over to every excess without fear of punishment imposed by the law, as they have no law and no justice which restrains them, or for lack of a spiritual minister to correct, instruct, and withdraw them from the license in which they are living, forming a small rabble, which is in no wise different from the savages.[55]

Perhaps Father Gibault himself considered the post at Ste. Genevieve a quite precarious, even dangerous, one for on September 8, 1782, he composed his last will. After invoking the Holy Trinity, as was customary, the missionary continued, "I, Pierre Gibault, diocesan priest of the diocese of Quebec, apostolic missionary and Vicar General in the Illinois Country, presently residing at Ste. Genevieve under the protection of His Christian Majesty, the king of Spain, being, by the grace of God, of sound mind and body, desiring to employ the remainder of my life preparing for death; considering what disposition should be made of the contents of the house I now occupy to be one of the principal matters about which I ought to render an account to God [of these possessions] furnished partly by the faithful and partly by my own wearisome toil, I am resolved to make my [last] will."[56] He directed that his body be buried without the customary elaborate obsequies attending the funeral of a priest. His library, a surprisingly large one, he bequeathed to his successor or to any priest willing to offer Masses for the repose of his soul.[57] His portable mass-kit, containing the necessary appurtenances for the celebration of Mass, was left to any priest agreeing to celebrate Mass for the repose of his soul each year on June 28, the feast of St. Peter the Apostle, whose name he bore. A mortgage which Gibault held on ". . . the property of both my brother Jacques and my uncle Antoine St. Jean, residing in the parish of the Assumption at St. Pierre du Portage, *gouvernement* of Montreal, is to be considered valueless and extinguished."[58] To his sister, Marie Louise, and her husband he bequeathed ". . . a negro named Laurent and a negress named Pelagie [Pelagria]." To Anne Perron, wife of Joseph Derocher, the priest willed a young negress named Marie Louise as a token of gratitude to Anne for keeping house for him, tending his garden, washing his clothes, and nursing him during his illnesses. Any debts which he might have contracted and not paid before his death were to be cared for. Whatever else remained in his house was to be sold at auction and the proceeds given his sister. In closing, the priest directed: "I name as my executors Monsieur François Le Cleve and Monsieur Jean Baptiste Prattie, traders and citizens of Ste. Genevieve, to whom I give jointly the advice to do everything necessary to execute this present will."[59] If Gibault was prompted to make his will because of ill health, he was two decades less twenty-three days removed from his demise.

Father Gibault's few years as pastor of the parish at Ste. Genevieve were not a period of contentment. He understood his French parishioners and their foibles which the Spanish bureaucratic officials, mostly fresh from Spain, found not only shocking but completely mystifying. Gibault, on the other hand, was equally puzzled by the Spanish officialdom. Writing to Louis-Philippe D'Esglis, the bishop of Quebec, some years after he had left Ste. Genevieve to settle at Vincennes, he described at some length his reaction to the Spanish governor of the Illinois Country:

> As to the rogueries of the commandant of Ste. Genevieve, he has no equal in the world. At the same time you will not find, perhaps, his equal for all sorts of good qualities. He has been commandant here for ten years and no one has had a single reproach against him, just, without partiality or exception for anyone, with no confederate either man or woman, disinterested to the last degree, solitary at home, full of religion himself and employing all his authority in having religion rigorously observed, fasting every Wednesday, and observing on that day an abstinence independent of other days, very benevolent, saying his breviary carefully every day, well educated and speaking good Latin; after all that what can one do when he is roguish? To remain quiet is all, for to save him is impossible. . . . You do not know the Spanish nation; for them all is despotism. If you do not go at their invitation, they send you an order which informs you that the welfare or the interest of His Majesty requires you at that moment for the government. What is one to do? One must withdraw as I did, in spite of advantages had from the king. . . .[60]

As his position at Ste. Genevieve became more distasteful to him, the heralded arrival of the Virginia commissioners, scheduled for the spring of 1783, offered Father Gibault an opportunity to recoup, he hoped, his financial reverses suffered in assisting George Rogers Clark and, perhaps, an opportunity to escape from the wooden bureaucracy of Spanish dominion back into the freer air of the totally French community. On March 4, 1783, the priest submitted a quite lengthy and very revealing memorial to the commissioners:

> Sirs, Although I have not the honor of being known to you, nor to the General Congress, it may be that you have been told something of my zeal for liberty and for the success of those who

have taken an interest in it and its defense. I have endangered and sacrificed everything for that cause, not only my property but several times even my life. I have exiled myself to take the part of the Americans against the Royalists; Should attention be paid only to the capture of Fort Vincennes on the Wabash my love for the cause of liberty will be recognized. I ask you, further, sirs, to consult with General Clark and all those, either officers or soldiers, who have served under him or after him for a trustworthy guarantee of my zeal. In spite of this I have been so ill-recompensed for my zeal that I have not been given a sou of indemnity for my sufferings, journeys, and fatigues, and the expenditures of these journeys, and I have not even been paid for the things necessary to sustain life, such as beeves, cows, and bacon of which I deprived myself to set a good example for my people, who have imitated me only too well to their great distress, being almost deprived of subsistence and of livelihood through giving all to the American troops. Persons have even killed several animals belonging to me which I would gladly have given them if they had asked for them instead of taking them by violence. Since I have always been ready to sacrifice myself it is improbable that I should have spared my property. They killed two of my cows, for which they have paid me not a penny except fine promises which are yet to be fulfilled. If I had profited by the necessitous conditions in which the American troops found themselves and sold dearer than the ordinary price, I should be wrong in demanding payment: but I gave my tithes of flour and corn at the same price that I would have sold them for ringing Spanish dollars on the other bank of the Mississippi, being more desirous of helping my country than an ally, and thinking moreover with confidence as did the Spaniards that these papers were worth really as much as piasters of silver or gold. Never should I have made these representations if the necessity and poverty into which the Americans have plunged us, myself and my people, had not made it impossible for me to keep silent. I pass in silence an almost infinite number of grievances, molestations, wrongs, and acts of violence of every kind which have almost completely ruined the country. It is not for me to inquire into the manner in which our commanders have behaved and of our commissioners who have governed us and have administered in military as well as civil affairs. Voluntary submission was always our rule of action. But it is for you, sirs, to inquire why and by whom we have been so inhumanly treated.

I send you herewith whatever I may have in records, accounts, and certificates of supplies furnished to the United States and especially to Virginia. I trust to your equity that I shall be justly paid. In addition my zeal will be the same and I shall always be satisfied with my judges and offer my prayers at all times for their prosperity and will ever style myself with respect,

Sirs

Your very humble and very obedient servant

Kaskaskia       Pierre Gibault, priest and
March 4th, 1783.     vicar general in the Illinois Country[61]

Gibault's effort was admirable, but neither he nor any other petitioner received redress from the state of Virginia.

A little less than a month after submitting his memorial to the Virginia commissioners, Father Gibault forwarded the first communication he apparently was able to send to the bishop of Quebec since the opening of hostilities at Kaskaskia in 1778. He wrote:

I have only a half an hour, if I seize the opportunity of sending a letter afforded me by Mr. Ducharme. In this short space I can only point out to your Lordship that I am always the same in working for the salvation of the people, except that age and weariness do not permit me as formerly to do what I would desire. The Reverend Father Bernard, Capuchin, serves the people of Cahokia as well as those of St. Louis where he lives. The Illinois people are more unfortunate than they were. After having been ruined and worn out by the Virginians and left without a commandant, without troops, and without justice, they are governing themselves by whim and caprice, or, to put it better, by the law of the strongest. We are expecting, however, in a short time, some troops with a commandant and a regulated court of justice. I hope to send your Lordship by Mr. Dubuque who will remain here some time, a detailed account, as far as I can, of all that has occurred within the last four or five years. I trust, likewise, that

106

through your paternal charity, you will not leave me longer without consolation. I have more need of it than ever, even though I have made it a principle to perform all my duties as if they were done in the presence of my Bishop; and since, consequently, you are always present to my eyes and to my spirit, it would be very agreeable to me to receive your instructions. While waiting for that good fortune I am, with all respect, submission and the most perfect obedience,

At Ste. Genevieve                    Your very humble servant,
April 1, 1783.                        P. Gibault, Priest.[62]

It is known that Father Gibault sent the promised letter detailing the events occurring in the Illinois Country between 1778 and 1783, but the document, unfortunately, did not survive. Only eighteen months after Gibault had written his letter to Briand, the bishop who knew the missionary best resigned the see of Quebec in favor of his coadjutor, Louis-Philippe D'Esglis. He assumed charge of the diocese on November 29, 1784. This latter's coadjutor was Jean-François Hubert, certainly no great admirer of Father Gibault. Changes of episcopal personnel as well as the rearrangement of diocesan lines to conform to new national boundaries presaged much trouble in the coming years for Pierre Gibault.

## STE. GENEVIEVE, VINCENNES,

## AND CAHOKIA

The successful conclusion of the American Revolution in favor of Great Britain's former colonies occasioned an essential modification of Catholic ecclesiastical authority which profoundly affected the life of Father Pierre Gibault. From 1634, when Father Andrew White and his Jesuit companions came to Maryland, until 1757, priests laboring in the English seaboard colonies, most of whom were Jesuits, exercised their ecclesiastical powers by virtue of authority granted them by their own Jesuit superior in England who received that authority directly from Rome. In 1757, Benjamin Petre, vicar apostolic of London and bishop of Prusa, a long suppressed episcopal see, assumed religious responsibility for all Catholics ". . . in the colonies and islands subject to the English crown in America."[1] Thenceforth until 1783 all Catholic ecclesiastics in the British colonies procured authority to administer the sacraments from the vicar apostolic of London. After 1783, when the former colonies became an independent nation, James Talbot, currently vicar apostolic of London and bishop of Birtha, declined to grant priests going to America any ecclesiastical faculties, declaring that he ". . . would exercise powers no longer over the American church."[2] For the moment, Talbot's quite churlish attitude was unimportant since Father John Lewis, superior of the Jesuits in English America until their suppression, was the validly appointed vicar-general of Talbot, who did not revoke that authority. But what would happen when Father Lewis died? Obviously, it behooved the clergy in the newly founded United States to obtain some sort of proper delegation directly from Rome. This they proceeded to seek under the leadership of Father John Carroll, a Jesuit until the dissolution of the order, the most able of the Catholic clergy in the new country.

Meeting at Whitemarsh, Maryland, on November 6, 1783, in a former, hallowed Jesuit residence, Fathers John Lewis, John Carroll, and three other priests framed a petition to the pope, Pius VI, requesting some form of independent ecclesiastical authority for their new country.[3] Within a surprisingly short time, considering the current difficulties of communication, the Roman authorities issued a decree, on June 9, 1784, appointing Father John Carroll prefect apostolic, or superior, ". . . of the missions in the thirteen United States of North America."[4] To indicate clearly that Carroll exercised authority independent of any intermediate jurisdiction, Talbot, vicar apostolic of London, was informed, on June 19, 1784, of the appointment of Carroll who was ". . . invested . . . with necessary and seasonable faculties, independent of any other ecclesiastical authority except the Sacred Congregation [of Propaganda] and that his Holiness intended, at the earliest possible moment, to establish a Bishop or a Vicar-Apostolic in that country."[5] Had the Roman officials been equally as careful to inform the bishop of Quebec that his jurisdiction no longer included the Illinois Country, life would have been much more simple for Father Gibault.

Though Father Gibault's "last will and testament" would indicate that he considered Ste. Genevieve a permanent, perhaps even final residence, within two years he removed to Vincennes.[6] What brought about the missionary's change of location cannot be explained by any presently available document. Perhaps Gibault found Spanish bureaucracy so annoyingly confining that he left the territory in disgust. Or, he may have so yearned to remain under the ecclesiastical jurisdiction of the bishop of Quebec that he went to Vincennes, hoping that thereby he might eventually be able to return to Canada. On abandoning the banks of the Mississippi, however, Gibault did not leave the Catholics of the area entirely without the services of a pastor. He was replaced by Father Paul de Saint Pierre.

Despite his French name, this priest was a German, born in the old duchy of Zweibrucken. His true name was Paul von Heiligenstein. Entering a French convent of the Discalced Carmelites, the young religious came to be known as Paul de Saint Pierre which, obviously, was a French translation of his German name.[7] In 1780, de Saint Pierre came to America as chaplain to one of the French regiments commanded by the comte de Rochambeau.[8] At the close of the war the French consul in Virginia urged de Saint Pierre to remain on the Atlantic seaboard, acting as chaplain to the French diplomatic corps. But the Carmelite yearned to become a missionary in the West.[9] Realizing his ambition in 1785, de Saint Pierre visited Vincennes whence he migrated to Kaskaskia and Cahokia.[10] Perhaps it was at Father Gibault's invitation that de Saint Pierre settled at Ste. Genevieve.[11] With Father de Saint Pierre at Ste. Genevieve and the

110

Capuchin Father Bernard de Limpach residing at St. Louis, Gibault could, in good conscience, leave the Mississippi Valley for Vincennes where the people desperately needed a pastor.

Since its establishment as a trading post in 1731, Vincennes had never enjoyed the presence of a resident pastor. The religious needs of its drifting population of French traders was supplied only sporadically by visits of missionaries who came at irregular intervals every few years. From a small village of ". . . sixty houses of French people . . ." in 1762, Vincennes grew quickly during the next two decades to a town containing upwards of 300 houses.[12] During those twenty years Vincennes received an influx of Americans and suffered from a total absence of effective civil government. Not only did Americans and French fail to harmonize but the American traders, illegally and most imprudently, supplied the aborigines with lavish quantities of alcoholic beverages as an inducement to gain control of the trade with the Indians.

John Filson, a noted traveler, who visited Vincennes in 1785 described conditions there thus:

> The Indians began to quarrel with the Americans and frequent murders ensued, this kind of Violence I found was no ways uncommon for a few days after I was Settled there a french man who lived near me was murdered, and laid at my door . . . the deed being done, no enquiry was made how he came by his death. . . . No people on earth live more chearfully than the people of this place balls and reveling take their nightly round, Vice and profanity become Common and habitual, the Court became in Some measure the ridicule of the people by a prostitution of their Characters to Gambling and Luxury which brought a general revolt from their authority.[13]

After residing at Vincennes for a year and a half, Pierre Gibault wrote to D'Esglis, bishop of Quebec, on June 6, 1786, describing moral conditions at Vincennes:

> I have enough confidence in our Lord Jesus Christ to hope to banish in a short time barbarism from Post Vincennes, where the in-

habitants, and especially the young people, have had no religious instruction for twenty-three years except when Mr. Payet or I happened to pass through there on our short missionary journeys. The inhabitants have been brought up like savages in the midst of whom they live.[14]

The major obstacle preventing the spiritual improvement of the people was the liquor traffic with the Indians which was forbidden by both civil and ecclesiastical law. Of this difficulty, Gibault remarked: "I should be well enough pleased with the spiritual condition of the people, were it not for that damnable trade in *eau-de-vie* which I cannot succeed in uprooting and which obliges me to refuse the sacraments to several, for the Indians commit horrible disorders when drunk, especially those of these nations here."[15]

Yet the experienced missionary was charitable in his judgment of his erring flock, explaining to the bishop:

In Canada all is civilized, here all is barbarous. You are in the midst of justice, here injustice dominates. There is no distinction from the greatest to the least except that of force. . . . Everybody is in poverty which engenders theft and rapine. Wantonness and drunkenness pass here as elegance and amusements quite in style. Breaking of limbs, murder by a dagger, saber or sword . . . are common and pistols and guns are but toys in these regions. And who has one to fear but the strongest. . . .[16]

For all their faults, the people themselves made sacrifices to retain Father Gibault, even though he spared ". . . nothing in order to set the faults of these sinners before their very eyes and openly . . ." rebuked them.[17] When the Cahokians beseeched the missionary to abandon Vincennes and settle with them, the parishioners at Vincennes:

. . . resolved unanimously to build a church ninety feet long and forty-two feet wide on a foundation with studwork, for which a part of the lumber has already been bought and also a few *toises* of stone for the foundation. The church will have pillars only seventeen feet high, but the winds are so fierce in this country that

even that is quite high for good strength. The house which serves
me now as a church will serve me as a rectory into which I intend
to move in a few months. The lot is large, very dry, and in the
middle of the village; it was I myself together with the *marguilliers*, who acquired this land sixteen years ago.[18]

At Vincennes, the question of the validity of ecclesiastical
jurisdiction concerned Father Gibault. During the previous winter he had received a communication from Father Ferdinand
Farmer, vicar-general of Father John Carroll at Baltimore,
granting Gibault authority to ". . . proclaim a jubilee, which
had been retarded by the war, to all the faithful Catholics of
America."[19] What puzzled the missionary was that, though the
letter was addressed to him as vicar-general of the bishop of
Quebec, he was granted an ecclesiastical privilege by an authority to whom he did not consider himself subject. "I would receive more willingly," he remarked to D'Esglis, "a suspension
from my bishop than honors from another."[20] Gibault was
equally puzzled by the presence of Father de Saint Pierre who
came to the area ". . . with some letters from the vicar general
granting him the privilege of ministering on the banks of the
Mississippi without mention of any place in particular. . . ."[21]
Gibault refrained from questioning the Carmelite's authority
without first having received directions from the bishop of Quebec. Nonetheless the problem remained. Who really had jurisdiction, the bishop of Quebec or the ecclesiastical authority at
Baltimore?

Father Gibault's lengthy missive of June 6, 1786, to the
Canadian bishop was, primarily, a defense of his missionary
life written in reply to a letter, no longer extant, from the bishop
which must have been sharply critical. Portions of Gibault's first
lengthy paragraph merit repetition.

> On receiving your letter, I made a general examination of
> my conscience regarding the complaints you mentioned. Hereby,
> I make the sincerest possible confession. First: since my mother's

113

death, I have had living with me a series of old men. I have sheltered four of them, each of whom died, one after another. During my frequent absences they nearly ruined me. They were not satisfied to stay with me any more than at any other place. Then Mr. and Mrs. de Montbrun lived with me for a year. She is my first cousin, a woman of advanced age. Why they left, I cannot say nor could I prevent it. But after they left I found myself lacking my curtains, my table linen, my clothes, my dishes and almost all of my pots and pans. Then I decided to board at a house near the church, which I did for two years. I neither liked it nor did I have enough money to pay $85 a month. [Then] I ate at home, employing a negress who was very untidy. After that I ate wherever I happened to be. I found an old man, aged ninety-eight, living in a shed, lacking food, heat, wood or blankets. . . . The shed had neither windows nor doors, though there was a foot of snow on the ground. The poor fellow, abandoned by everyone, a stranger, had a horrible cancer at the nape of his neck. You can imagine what compassion the sight of such misfortune aroused in me since I knew that at Post Vincennes he had been well off, having sold his holdings for $450 in American silver. . . . Now he was dying with only the priest. I brought him some wood and corn, something to ease his cancer, a buffalo robe to cover him. As I was leaving the next morning for Prairie du Rocher, St. Philippe and Cahokia, to be absent a month or more, I told his daughter to move into my house so that she would not lack a place for her father. In other words, she was mistress of the house, which was not commonly known at the time. . . . When I came back, I found the arrangement so useful, inside and out, that it was as though my mother was still alive. Then her husband went down to New Orleans [planning] to return the following summer. He did what so many ingrate Canadians do who marry and abandon their wives in the [Illinois] country. Over the years I have received over thirty letters from wives or their pastors seeking to find their husbands without success. These [two people] are not separated, as you say in your letter. Her fondest wish is the return of her husband. My kindness to her is really a safeguard. Perhaps this gives rise to scandal, as you say, but it could also be that people down here are suspicious of anyone on good terms with the pastor, without considering how much trouble they give him. Sensible persons, with whom I consulted, advise my

ignoring the supposed scandal and keeping her in my home until
her husband returns. You speak of her as a young woman. You
know little about the climate of this area. A Creole is older at
thirty-five than a Canadian at fifty-five. She has all the qualities
of a prudent Christian [woman]. She is no more attractive than
her background would [tend to] make her. . . . You chide me for
removing to Post Vincennes despite my promise made to M.
Payet. And there are other faults of which I am accused. I am
charged with leaving my station at Ste. Genevieve and its dependencies [its mission stations] to procure a better income.
Whoever said that knows nothing about the character of Post
Vincennes. . . . They did not tell you that I spent four months at
the home of M. De Gras while I sought other quarters. Where else
could I go; there was no rectory. . . . Fortunately, [eventually]
I found a small room with a German who acted as my domestic. I
do not recount these details to justify myself, but simply to inform you. Returning to the point for a moment, you know that I
have seen every parish from Kamouraska . . . and St. Paul Bay
in the south [the lower reaches of the St. Lawrence] to Michilimackinac in the north. I met no pastor who did not have living
with him his mother, sister, cousins or some ladies and their
daughters who cared for his house. You yourself have some wid-
ows and orphans. I fail to understand why this is proper [there]
but not so among the Illinois or at Post Vincennes; how it is
[considered] a terrible scandal [here] while no one takes offense
at it in Canada, but regard it, rather, as necessary. How am I to
understand your letter which says that it is a scandal to the whole
diocese for a pastor to have a woman reside in his house as being
contrary to church law and the synodal statutes of the diocese? I
fail to see the difference since one knows that this custom is permitted in Canada but is intolerable elsewhere.[22]

Disposing, thus, of criticism leveled at his domestic arrangements, Father Gibault took up, one by one, the several
other complaints contained in the bishop's communication. In
doing so the harassed priest submitted a portrait of a zealous,
devoted, charitable pastor. Charged with having the reputation
of indulging to excess in spirituous liquor, Gibault responded
by detailing his normal daily activities. Though poorly nour-

ished and inadequately housed, he cared for his people, even to giving daily catechism lessons to the children as well as teaching the boys to read and write. Further, sick or well, no matter what grave dangers threatened from weather or hostile Indians, he never failed to undertake difficult journeys bringing the consolations of religion to those in need. Such zealous devotion to duty could scarcely be expected from an indolent inebriate.[23]

In replying to the bishop's inference that he was becoming aged, feeble, nearly blind, and unable longer to serve his people, Father Gibault, rather testily replied: "I feel as well as I ever did. I am capable of making the same journeys I always did. I have no pain whatever, and I never had any, not even a toothache. Perhaps they thought that because I no longer go fishing and hunting as I formerly did, that old age caused this, but it is my tastes which have changed. In fact, having devoted myself altogether to the instruction of youth, to reforming the manners and bad habits of a large village almost barbarous, to travelers and merchants who come here from all parts of America, and to other daily exercises of the ministry, would these permit me to do what I did formerly?"[24]

Once more the charge of treason for his part in the submission of Vincennes reared its head and again Gibault denied having any responsibility for the matter. He emphatically declared that he had accompanied Dr. Laffont and the Americans to Vincennes only because a well-armed expedition offered a favorable opportunity for paying the town a visit, pointing out that he had been unable to do so for quite some time. As proof of his innocence, Gibault forwarded to the bishop Laffont's letter, previously quoted in full, testifying to the priest's purely spiritual functions in that much debated affair.[25]

Concluding his defense with a tone of resignation, as though he hardly hoped to be believed, Father Gibault declared:

And what will you infer from all I may have been able to say to you? It is almost impossible for you to penetrate the truth. They

116

told you certain things, I tell you almost the contrary. You neither know these regions nor the manners and vices of those who inhabit them. . . . You may conclude what you wish, as for me these are my conclusions.

I shall withdraw into my house, as soon as it is finished, with my beadle and a small boy; then may God grant that slandering may cease . . . , but I doubt it. At the same time, I beg you to remember that I am all alone, abandoned to myself. . . .[26]

In spite of the bishop's obvious lack of confidence in him, a burden which a less zealous apostle would hardly have carried so well, Pierre Gibault patiently continued his work, and with gratifying results, as the parish records of the Old Cathedral at Vincennes amply demonstrate. Before the new church was completed, François Bosseron, a prominent citizen, donated a bell for its steeple and paid the cost of transporting it from Philadelphia. On December 3, 1785, the feast of St. Francis Xavier, patron of the parish, Father Gibault blessed the bell and dutifully recorded its "baptism," naming it Marie Françoise in honor of the donor's daughter.[27] Other significant consolations came to Gibault, such as the reception into the Church, on February 3, 1786, of the wife and five children of one Peter Waldren, a Catholic whose family had previously received no religious instruction.[28] The incident would signify that Gibault's relationship to Americans settling at Vincennes was prospering.

Father Gibault's difficulties with ecclesiastical superiors was far from over. He was soon brought face to face with the anomalous situation arising between the bishop of Quebec and Father John Carroll of Baltimore. Informed from Rome of his responsibility for the whole area of the new United States, Carroll, with some reluctance, sent Father Pierre Huet de la Valinière as his vicar-general for the area west of the Allegheny Mountains to the eastern bank of the Mississippi, warning his appointee, however, not to impugn Father Gibault's authority. Few clerics have equaled the arrogant imprudence of that misguided man. Born in France on January 10, 1732, de la Valinière came to Canada in 1754 and was ordained at Montreal on June 15, 1755. Fiery, self-willed, and turbulent, he was constantly moved from parish to parish because of his inability to get along with people. In 1779 de la Valinière was expelled from Canada for aiding the American invasion force. Shipped to England as a prisoner, he was released after a year. Then he returned to France and volunteered as a chaplain for the French forces sent to aid the American cause. Though he apparently did not serve as a chaplain, he reached the United States in 1785 and made his way back to Canada, hoping again to labor in the diocese of Quebec. Refusing to employ that stormy petrel, the bishop, most imprudently gave the man a letter of recommendation which de la Valinière used to obtain ecclesiastical employment under Father John Carroll. During the summer of 1786 de la Valinière reached Kaskaskia.[29]

Father de la Valinière barely settled in at Kaskaskia before he incited unrest. During an altercation with Father Paul de Saint Pierre, the irascible vicar-general publicly cast doubts on the validity of the latter's priestly ordination, but by October 17, 1786, the accusation was retracted.[30] Returning to the lists the following spring, on April 11, 1787, the vicar-general addressed a public letter to the parishioners of Father de Saint Pierre's parish at Cahokia vilifying the Carmelite and threatening to report him to the federal congress.[31] Eleven days later, on April 22, 1787, the people of Cahokia sent a curt, caustic reply, vehemently defending their pastor and flatly declared that thenceforth they would not recognize de la Valinière as having any ecclesiastical authority over them. Soon the parishioners at Kaskaskia were up in arms against the contentious vicar-general. On September 21, 1787, they presented him with a lengthy list of formal charges. Their document concluded:

> In consequence of these facts & a great number of others which we pass over in Silence, the Underwritten are of opinion that M. De la Valinière is a perturbator of the public peace, a

dangerous man by the fury of his disposition, the theocratic despotism with which he wishes to govern us, the violence of his passions, & the maxims which he strives to establish & which we judge contrary to the American Constitution, to Sound reason and good morals.[32]

What relationship existed between de la Valinière and Father Gibault is not clearly evident, though it could hardly have been amicable. In September 1787 Father de Saint Pierre, writing to Barthelemi Tardiveau, an Illinois congressman, remarked:

> After all you know the troubles in which M. de la Valinière throws M. Gibault, the best inhabitants of Kas[kaskia], Kaos [Cahokia], Prairie du Rocher, has thrown and throws every day, how he deranges the good intelligence with the Spanish priests our neighbors. Render us, I beseech you, the service of exposing the whole to the Honorable Congress, that they may please oblige M. John Carroll, Prefect Apostolic, to take all ecclesiastical powers from him if he has given him any, & drive him out of our country & confirm M. Gibault in his former office of Vicar General, which he has always exercised with honor & satisfaction to his brethren, our neighbors, and all Christians. It is also well known how he exerted himself for Congress at all times.[33]

Perhaps seeing the handwriting on the wall, Father de la Valinière, on May 26, 1787, wrote to the bishop of Quebec pleading for permission to return to Canada ". . . to some little parish that you could give me, provided I could be useful in the salvation of souls, . . ."[34] Even in that supposedly humble missive de la Valinière could not refrain from making one parting thrust. ". . . the enemy of our salvation pursues me and troubles me here. A Carmelite without letters of priesthood has come here and is arousing the people to insurrection, and M. Gibault continues always the conduct which is known to you."[35] De la Valinière left the Illinois Country, probably in 1788, and settled at Split Rock, New York, among some French Canadians living there. Within a few years his unfortunate character again forced him to flee. He returned to Canada and ended his days at Repentigny where he was killed in an accident on June 29, 1806.[36]

Perhaps de la Valinière's contentiousness in the Illinois Country had the good effect of helping to clarify the territorial lines between the diocese of Quebec and the ecclesiastical authority in the United States. By some means Father Carroll learned that Bishop Hubert of Quebec was concerned to discover that the American seemed to be exercising jurisdiction in an area traditionally a part of the diocese of Quebec. Writing to Hubert, on May 5, 1788, Carroll explained that he took an active interest in the Illinois Country because he believed, in good faith, that the area had been confided to him by the Holy See. While Carroll would be grateful, he wrote, if Hubert were willing to supply priests for the Illinois Country, he doubted that the American government would take kindly to any British subject exercising even spiritual authority in the new country. In passing Father Carroll remarked: ". . . reports have reached me concerning M. Gibault's conduct that are very unfavorable to him."[37] The brief reference to Gibault is important because it characterizes Carroll's consistent attitude to the missionary and may well explain why, not too many years later, Father Gibault chose to settle at New Madrid rather than to contend with what perhaps was a preconceived opinion.

Before Bishop Hubert replied to Father Carroll's letter, he received a very touching communication from Pierre Gibault. Because it is Gibault's last extant communication to the bishop of Quebec, it deserves to be quoted in full.

> It seems to me by your silence that you have forgotten even to send an answer to some matters which necessarily cause me some embarrassment, and concerning which a clarification from you should not be so long delayed.[38] The wretched condition in which, some two or three years ago you thought me to be, ought to have given you enough compassion not to forget entirely a priest who has not ceased for a single moment of his life to sacri-

120

fice not only his pleasures and rest but also to expose his own life to the fury of the barbarians, in order to fulfill his ministry with the same views and with the same intentions with which he made the sacrifice between the hands of his bishop. There was no reason for expecting this neglect, since I have removed without difficulty whatever might have given cause for suspicion, however unjust, of my manner of living. It has been over a year since I have any liquor in my house, and I do not even drink a swallow now and then, either of wine or of brandy. I think no longer about it. It is not a vow, nor is it a sacrifice; for, whatever may have been related to you, I never had any attachment for any kind of drink, and never did more than drink a swallow of brandy, as travelers will, not even thinking about it when I had none. It must be that those who told you abominations so atrocious as those you mention in your last letter were incited by the father of lies, or it must be that I reproved them too strongly concerning their vices and bad conduct, for I do not see any other cause for their calumny. It would be useless to repeat what I said to you with such detail in my last letter. It would be much better for me to be under your very eyes than so far away. I beg you, therefore, to consider that for the last twenty years I have been continuously serving in these regions without having a fixed place of abode so to speak, that I have been almost always on the road, in all seasons of the year, always running the risk of being massacred by the barbarians, as a number of persons have been on these same roads. Even M. Paul Desruisseaux, whom you must have known at Quebec, was killed and M. Bonvouloir was wounded so near me that I was all covered by his blood. My age of more than fifty-one years, the need I have of being better sheltered, after so many hardships which inevitably accompany so many journeys and long trips, the repugnance I have in serving another bishop either in Spain or in republican America, and a thousand other reasons, all these, I say, well considered, lead me to expect from your generosity my recall, which I ask of you at once and on my knees, and in this I believe I am following the will of God who inspires me for my own salvation. And as for opposition to me because of the fear that I may have been or was active for the American Republic, you have only to reread my first letter in which I give you an account of our capture, and my last letter in which I sent you a certificate of my conduct at Post

Vincennes, in the capture of which they said I had taken a hand; and you will see that not only did I not meddle with anything, but on the contrary I have always regretted and do regret every day the loss of the mildness of British rule. As for the spiritual succor of the people in these regions, I can assure you that they will lack less than heretofore, for they have a priest at Kaskaskia, another one at Cahokia, and they would not be long without one at Post Vincennes were I to leave, since it is the post favored by Congress.

Thus, Monseigneur, all conspires to make me hope for my recall, and the sooner the better, for the time which separates the fulfillment from the desire is always long. I earnestly hope for it, and I shall sacrifice the rest of my days in showing you my gratitude for it. It is with this hope that I have the honor to be, Monseigneur, your Lordship's

|  | Very humble, very obedient and |
| At Post Vincennes | very submissive servant, |
| May 22, 1788. | P. Gibault, Priest.[39] |

Even today, nearly two hundred years after it was written, Father Gibault's letter engenders sympathy for a man who spent twenty grueling years laboring so earnestly in an unrewarding apostolic vineyard. Since 1772, for sixteen long years, Gibault had received hardly a word of praise or encouragement from his superior. That year, the bishop informed the missionary that people were discontented with their pastor because he was absent so frequently as well as because he supposedly did not conduct himself with the reserve and decorum expected of the clergy. In 1775, completely discouraged, Gibault begged to be recalled to Canada. If his conduct was a source of scandal, Bishop Briand could well have recalled his subject at that time. Further, if the charge were true, the bishop should have withdrawn Gibault. By 1776, Briand was apparently so concerned about Gibault that he requested Father Meurin for a confidential report. If Meurin's reply was objectively correct, that Gibault was causing scandal by keeping very late hours, gaming with the young men, and imbibing to excess, these were undoubtedly adequate rea-

122

sons, even cogent ones, for promptly ordering Pierre Gibault to return to Canada and at once. All of the bishop's complaints had been answered, time and again, by Father Gibault. Perhaps nothing so clearly demonstrates the missionary's unquenchable zeal, his heroic devotion to duty, as does his simple constancy through the most crushing adversity, lack of understanding on the part of his superior. Left without any clerical companionship for long years, unappreciated by his bishop, often misunderstood by his people, it is a wonder that the harassed missionary did not abandon it all. Yet he stayed at his post, year after year, striving to accomplish his task. Bishop Briand's successors, especially Hubert, were coldly critical of Gibault. To Hubert, Father Gibault was the typical dog with the bad name. And that name was passed on by Hubert to John Carroll at Baltimore.

Bishop Hubert answered Carroll's letter of May 5, 1788, informing the American that as far as he knew the Illinois Country had not been officially removed from the jurisdiction of the diocese of Quebec. However, having no priests available to take charge of the area, Hubert would be pleased if Carroll would assume responsibility for it. As to Carroll's inquiry regarding Father Gibault, Hubert dismissed the missionary with cold indifference, not even damning him with faint praise.

> True it is that M. Gibault was nominated twenty years ago as vicar general for the Illinois country; but since that time the episcopal see of Quebec has twice changed its incumbent without his faculties having been renewed. Complaints of different kinds, especially a suspicion of treason toward the government, caused my predecessors to entertain some antipathy towards him, so much so that I propose to give him no employment for the future. That would be easier for you to do. . . .
>
> I received a letter from him this year in which he asks to come back to the Province of Quebec. After the disadvantageous opinion that the government has formed of him, I can not prudently consent to his return. Nevertheless, if you judge it proper

to continue him as a missionary, I ratify in advance all that you may be pleased to ordain therein, either in regard to him or to other missionaries now there or to be sent.[40]

This ended, effectively, Pierre Gibault's relationship to the diocese of Quebec. In effect, the long-suffering missionary was abandoned, left to an ecclesiastical superior who had no more understanding of the difficulties encountered by a priest on a raw frontier than did the bishop of Quebec.

At that crucial moment, Pierre Gibault again found himself the only priest readily available to the people inhabiting the villages on the east bank of the Mississippi, from Cahokia to Kaskaskia. To no one's regret, Pierre Huet de la Valinière departed from Kaskaskia in 1789. During the same year, Father Paul de Saint Pierre, much beloved pastor at Cahokia, transferred to Ste. Genevieve. A shadowy figure, Father Le Dru, a Dominican, settled briefly at Kaskaskia, but left there in November 1789.[41] Under those circumstances, Father Gibault had little choice except to return to the Mississippi Valley villages since the larger population there could hardly be left to the precarious sacerdotal care of the pastors of St. Louis and Ste. Genevieve. Gibault left Vincennes soon after October 11, 1789, which is the date of his last entry in the parish records of the Old Cathedral at Vincennes. His first entry at Cahokia was November 12, 1789. At least one old friend, François Vigo, had a kind word for Father Gibault, saying that the missionary was ". . . a true pastor wholly devoted to his people and his duty as a priest."[42]

Comparatively speaking, Cahokia was a peaceful enclave in the midst of the turmoil inflicting the villages of the Illinois Country after its conquest by George Rogers Clark. Joseph Labuxière, state's attorney and notary, who had been in the Illinois Country since 1751, reported to Congress, on July 17, 1786: "The misunderstandings of the magistrates of Kaskaskia and the extreme disorder of the business of the individuals, oc-

124

casioned by some persons greedy for money, have compelled me to withdraw with my family to Cahokia where I have found the inhabitants filled with unity of peace and fidelity to the states, and a court of justice which they are careful to administer with equity to those who ask its help."[43] The fortunate atmosphere at Cahokia may be attributed to several diverse factors. Under French dominion, the area surrounding the village of Cahokia had been granted as a seigneury to the priests of the Missions-Etrangères who had been able to grant lands to families of their own selection. Resultantly, settlers were, for the most part, stable heads of families, industrious farmers seeking a solid, peaceful existence. Further, as various census reports taken after 1779 clearly demonstrate, the population of Cahokia remained almost wholly French.[44] Those of Anglo-Saxon lineage seeking homes near Cahokia settled at Grand Ruisseau not far from Cahokia, but also not a part of the French village. Then, the Cahokians, old hands at trading with the Indians, were too experienced to allow their dusky neighbors any access to alcoholic beverages, knowing full well what calamities followed upon that disastrous practice. Hence the people of Cahokia passed several ordinances prohibiting the sale of eau de vie to the aborigines and, when observance was slack, they strengthened the penalties imposed on those who dared violate the regulations.[45]

An important factor in maintaining public order at Cahokia certainly must have been the fairly regular presence of a resident pastor, who, for the greater part of two decades, was usually a man whom the people deeply respected. Father Sebastien Meurin, retiring to Cahokia on the arrival of Pierre Gibault at Kaskaskia in 1768, served Cahokia constantly until his death in 1777. From that year, until the arrival of Father Paul de Saint Pierre, in 1785, the Capuchin pastor of St. Louis, Father Bernard de Limpach, called at Cahokia quite regularly, keeping the Cahokians religiously alive. The profound devotion of the Cahokians to Father de Saint Pierre was all too clearly demonstrated in 1787 by their vehement defense of their pastor in the face of the unwarranted attacks by de la Valinière. Though the Cahokians, in a petititon submitted by them to Congress on July 16, 1786, were sharply critical of Father Gibault's sale of property which they considered as their own, they, nevertheless, invited him to return there in 1789 when Father de Saint Pierre accepted the pastorate of Ste. Genevieve on the western bank of the Mississippi. Thus, while Kaskaskia, for example, lacked consistent spiritual guidance, Cahokia, on the contrary, rarely suffered from a lack of dedicated spiritual direction between 1768 and 1789.

Before leaving Vincennes, Father Gibault wrote two letters to Father Carroll, by then bishop-elect of Baltimore, reporting in detail on conditions. On January 20, 1790, Carroll replied in such manner as to offer little consolation to the grizzled missionary, then sixty-three:

> It happened, very unfortunately for the affairs of your church as well as for my pleasure, that the bearers of your letters of June 16 and July 28 [1789] arrived and departed here during my absence. You wrong M. de la Valinière by imputing to him alone the accusations of which I made mention in my former letter. Travelers who returned to Philadelphia from Kaskaskia had mentioned these things even before his departure from there, and without knowing who was the priest whom these accusations particularly concerned. I had commanded him, at the time of his departure from Philadelphia, to send me some information on this subject. Since that time, I have received from different sources the accounts of which I informed you in my last letter. In fact I regret to tell you that Monseigneur the Bishop of Quebec in a letter, which he has written to me, called to my notice that his predecessors had thought during the last years that they ought not to confide so much in you for all that part of the West as they had formerly done.[46]

In the light of Carroll's expressed attitude it is surprising that in the same letter the American ecclesiastic requested Father

126

Gibault to inform him concerning the whereabouts and conduct of both Father Le Dru and Father de Saint Pierre. Concerning the first, Carroll remarked: ". . . the conduct of this monk in Acadia . . . weigh me down with sorrow and make me blame my too great readiness in giving him power even for a very limited time."[47] As to the admirable de Saint Pierre, Carroll noted: "I am worried about M. de Saint Pierre. He left here without any power to administer the sacraments, for at that time I possessed no right to get it to him; and since his departure I have been unable to make up my mind to send him that power, because I am in no wise assured that he came to America with the consent of the superiors of his order or with such approbation as the usages of ecclesiastical discipline require."[48]

Since Father Gibault must have been aware, by the summer of 1789, that John Carroll was shortly to be consecrated a bishop with authority over the whole of the new United States, including the area north of the Ohio, the future bishop's communication could not have engendered much hope in Gibault's mind for the security of his future under a superior who, apparently, had already prejudged him. However, life had to go on. And the Illinois Country was, finally, about to receive the civil stability which it had not enjoyed for a quarter of a century.

The Northwest Ordinance of 1787, which gave governmental form and substance to the area north of the Ohio and east of the Mississippi, was finally implemented in the Illinois Country with the arrival at Kaskaskia of Governor Arthur St. Clair on March 5, 1790. Acting without delay, the governor proclaimed the boundaries of St. Clair county on April 27, establishing three judicial districts, one of which was Cahokia. On March 7, only two days after his arrival, St. Clair addressed himself to the problem of land tenure by issuing a directive requiring all inhabitants to prove claim to any land each held under the federal congressional act of 1788 granting all Frenchmen a bounty of 400 acres in compensation for injuries suffered during the Revolution.[49] The order, while quite necessary in establishing titles to land, immediately brought to light some insuperable difficulties. Not only had none of the land in the area been previously surveyed, but there was no one in the territory competent to make the survey. Further, people were so poor that they would be unable to pay for the service. Besides, the French deeply resented the legal necessity of proving title to land which, in many cases, had been held by the same family for generations.

Under the leadership of Father Pierre Gibault, the people of Cahokia, Kaskaskia, and Prairie du Rocher memorialized Governor St. Clair, praying him to consider their problem.[50] Pointing out their obvious poverty as well as calling attention to all of their sufferings in the cause of freedom they besought the governor to find some other solution for their difficulty.

Striving to assist the people, Governor St. Clair reported to Congress, pointing out the impracticality of the means legislated for clarifying land titles in St. Clair county.[51] Concurrently, the governor submitted a report to President Washington, including with it a series of petitions from various persons requesting grants of land. One of these was a request by Father Gibault asking for the grant of ". . . small piece of land that has been in the occupation of the priests at Cahokia for a long time . . . he wishes to possess it in propriety. It is true that he was very useful to General Clark upon many occasions, and has suffered very considerable losses; I believe no injury would be done to any one by his request being granted, but it was not for me to give away the lands of the United States."[52] Accompanying the petition (as was the case with the others) was a lengthy explanation by Gibault, detailing his sufferings and losses in the cause of the Revolution, his loyalty to the United States, and explaining that the small piece of land besought for himself was chiefly requested as a bulwark against utter poverty in his old age.[53]

If he but knew the reaction his request would cause from Bishop Carroll, Gibault would undoubtedly have gladly forgone submitting his humble petition. On learning of the missionary's effort, the bishop wrote, on January 23, 1792, ". . . I saw in the month of March of last year, the announcement of a law passed by the Congress of the United States, by which certain possessions, hitherto ecclesiastic, is transferred to you to be your private and particular property; . . . I should like to be instructed concerning this. . . ."[54] If Carroll's displeasure at Gibault's action was not evident from his letter to the latter, it certainly was in a communication the American bishop sent to Bishop Hubert of Quebec. "Last year," Carroll reported, "M. Gibault and some other persons, by means of a statement which I regard as false, obtained the grant of some ecclesiastical property at Kaskaskia and at Post Vincennes. I am taking steps to have that grant invalidated."[55]

Bishop Carroll's letter of January 23, 1792, to Gibault contained one sentence which was, in effect, the handwriting on the wall. Carroll informed the aging missionary: ". . . I am in the hope of receiving soon some helpers to aid you in your laborious duties, and it is important to preserve for you, for them, and for your successors the possessions of the Church."[56] Within the new diocese of Baltimore a new broom was obviously sweeping clean. Clerical associates on the still raw frontier might have been welcome to Pierre Gibault a decade ago, but now he was aging, out of favor with a new superior whom he had never met, and perhaps simply too tired to face the inevitable adjustment that the arrival of young, inexperienced, though certainly zealous, priests would bring. Rather than facing the adjustment which could only lead to further misunderstandings, was it not better to depart for Spanish territory? Late in 1789, John Rice Jones, writing to General Hamtramck, remarked: "I am informed that Mr. Gibault is to have the offer of the cure of

*L'Anse a la Graise,* where there is a commanding officer and 20 soldiers newly arrived from New Orleans."[57] The information was accurate for, after bearing the heat and the labor of the day in the Illinois Country for just two years short of a quarter century, Pierre Gibault accepted the invitation from the Spaniards and moved to New Madrid where he lived out the years left to him.

FINAL YEARS AT NEW MADRID

For the French in the Mississippi Valley living under Spanish domination would prove a nettlesome experience. The Treaty of Fontainebleu of November 3, 1762, was two years old before the people whom it chiefly affected were officially informed that they had become subjects of His Catholic Majesty, Carlos III of Spain. From the official communication informing them of their new status the French in the Mississippi Valley had some basis for hoping that life would continue much as before. Louis XV informed Jean Jacques Blaise Dabbadie, director general of the colony of Louisiana: "I hope . . . for the advantage and tranquillity of the inhabitants of the colony of

Louisiana . . . that he [the king of Spain] will be pleased to give orders to his governor or any other officer employed at his service in the said colony . . . that the ecclesiastics . . . shall continue to perform their function . . . ; that the judges of ordinary jurisdiction as well as the Superior Council shall continue to administer justice according to the law, forms and usages of the colony. . . ."[1] For the following two years the colony continued to be governed by French officials for Spain appeared in no hurry to assume control of its newly acquired possession.

Finally, on March 5, 1766, Don Antonio de Ulloa, a distinguished scientist, but a particularly inept civil administrator, arrived, with a small military force, to assume control of the colony. Instead of residing at New Orleans and taking possession of the colony in a formal, public ceremony, Ulloa tarried at La Balize, ruling the colony through a Frenchman, Captain Charles Philippe Aubry who succeeded to authority at the death of Dabbadie on February 4, 1765.[2] Though Ulloa made no drastic changes in the government of the colony, he alienated the French merchants by issuing severely restrictive regulations. Revolting against Spain's representative, the French at New Orleans expelled Ulloa from the colony on November 1, 1768. When that news reached Spain the crown sent Don Alejandro O'Reilly at the head of 3,000 troops to take command of the colony.[3] Disembarking at New Orleans on August 17, 1769, the new governor took formal possession of Louisiana and quite as quickly crushed opposition to the Spanish crown by summarily executing, on October 25, 1769, five of the ringleaders of the revolt and exiling several others to Cuba.

Having thus effectively gained control of the colony, O'Reilly proceeded to organize it along lines customary in other colonial possessions of the king of Spain. A cabildo of six regidors replaced the French Superior Council while proper local officials were appointed to manage civil affairs. In each district outside of New Orleans an army officer was stationed as both military and civil ruler. O'Reilly also issued an abridgment of the civil and criminal code prevailing in other Spanish colonies. Therein the intimate relationship between Spain's civil government and the Church appears all too clearly. Condign punishment by the state was legislated for blasphemy, adultery, prostitution, and other violations of Christian morality.[4] While the Spanish crown by long tradition employed the Church as an arm of the state, at least the Church was supported financially from public funds rather than by tithes collected from the people.

The transfer of civil and military control of Louisiana to Spain was quickly followed by a similar change in ecclesiastical jurisdiction. Since the beginning of the eighteenth century the area had been the responsibility of the bishop of Quebec who delegated his authority to a resident vicar-general. At O'Reilly's suggestion, the colony was attached to the diocese of Santiago de Cuba.[5] In 1772, Jaime José de Echeverria, bishop of Santiago de Cuba, assumed jurisdiction over Louisiana by sending thither Father Cyrillo de Barcelona, a Spanish Capuchin, with four Capuchin companions, who was appointed the bishop's vicar-general.[6] Confusion immediately resulted as well as ill feeling because Father Dagobert de Longuory, a French Capuchin, had been for many years vicar-general of the bishop of Quebec and was extremely well liked by the people.[7] The anomalous ecclesiastical situation was solved in 1782 when Rome, at the request of Spain, appointed Father Cyrillo bishop of Tricali, an extinct see in Greece, and auxiliary bishop of the see of Santiago de Cuba with authority over Louisiana where he was directed to reside.[8] Bishop Cyrillo, and his successor, Luis Peñalver y Cardinas, directed his attention to New Orleans and other villages within easy reach of the capital, but neither he nor his successor ventured northward, leaving ecclesiastical matters exclusively in the hands of local military commandants.

After the American Revolution Spanish colonial officials realized that it was unwise to neglect the northern stretches of

Louisiana. Martin Navarro, intendant during the governorship of Estevan Miró (1785-1789), warned the home government that if Spain hoped to retain the colony of Louisiana she should pursue a policy of encouraging migration of Anglo-Saxons from the east, offering such attractive terms that many would be willing to become subjects of the king of Spain.[9] Otherwise the Americans within reach of the Mississippi River were bound to invade Louisiana and eventually annex it to the United States. To avert such a disaster, Don Diego de Gardoqui, chargé d'affaires for Spain in the United States, was instructed to make every effort to encourage Americans to emigrate to Louisiana.[10] Possibly through a mutual friend, Thomas Hutchins, Gardoqui offered a large tract of land to Colonel George Morgan, who had but recently failed to negotiate the purchase of land on the east bank of the Mississippi for the ambitious New Jersey Land Company.[11]

George Morgan, orphaned son of a reasonably prosperous Philadelphia merchant, was apprenticed at thirteen to the firm of Baynton and Wharton, also Philadelphia merchants.[12] Becoming a partner in 1763, Morgan managed the company's business at Kaskaskia, residing there intermittently between 1765 and 1772. When that company failed, Morgan opened his own firm at Philadelphia, but spent much time and money speculating in western lands. During the Revolution, Morgan held the office of Indian agent with headquarters at Fort Pitt. Continuing his interest in western lands after the Revolution, Morgan organized the New Jersey Land Company which sought to purchase from the federal government a tract stretching along the Mississippi, including within it most of the old French settlements. When Congress required more money per acre than the New Jersey group was willing to pay, the project was abandoned.[13] At that juncture, Gardoqui, becoming acquainted with Morgan, suggested that Spain would gladly grant him a land concession on the western bank of the Mississippi.

Morgan proposed to establish what would have been a state within a state. Subject to approval by the crown, Gardoqui offered Morgan a tract stretching 300 miles along the Mississippi River from the mouth of the Arkansas to Cape St. Cosme in the present Perry County, Missouri, and extending far enough westward to include some 15,000,000 acres.[14] Those who migrated, though obliged to swear allegiance to the crown of Spain, were to have authority to make their own laws, elect their own officials, and enjoy complete liberty of conscience. Advertising his project widely, Morgan, with seventy recruits, set out from Fort Pitt in January 1789 and in April of that year chose the site at New Madrid as the center around which the colony was to develop.[15] In May 1789 Morgan visited New Orleans to confer with Governor Miró, who treated the American considerately but strongly opposed Morgan's plans, at least under the conditions tentatively granted by Gardoqui. Spain, declared Miró, welcomed immigrants, but all must accept Spain's laws, including that forbidding the public practice of any but the Catholic faith. Hastening to consolidate Spain's control of the area under discussion, Miró, on July 28, 1789, appointed Pedro Foucher commandant at the nearly nonexistent New Madrid.[16] Shortly, Morgan lost interest in the project and the Americans whom he induced to settle near New Madrid drifted off. Yet the little village survived.

Permanent settlers at New Madrid were, for the most part, former residents of Vincennes or of the old French villages along the eastern bank of the Mississippi. A census taken in 1791 shows, for example, that the total population of New Madrid was 220. Forty-five heads of families were from Vincennes, four were from Kaskaskia, four from St. Louis, and one from Ste. Genevieve.[17] Six years later, in 1797, New Madrid had a population of 569 plus 46 slaves, 130 horses, and 777 cows. Of the 166 family names listed in the census 60 were typically Anglo-Saxon while all of the others were French, except a few which were Spanish.[18] By 1799 a census showed the population of New Madrid to be 782. Strangely, within that brief two-year interval the number of Anglo-Saxon names had declined to 20.[19]

When the establishment of New Madrid could hardly have been more than a rumor, Father Paul de Saint Pierre, then pastor at Cahokia, wrote to Bishop Cyrillo, on May 1, 1787: "A new establishment has been begun a little below the entrance of the Beautiful River [the Ohio]. They will need a pastor who knows English and German. I offer myself for this place."[20] De Saint Pierre did not receive that post, but instead was appointed to Ste. Genevieve. Pierre Gibault, who was offered the pastoral care of New Madrid, remained at Cahokia until late in the year 1791 or early 1792.[21] Early that year Bishop Carroll sent Father Michael Levadoux, a Sulpician lately arrived from France, to be his vicar-general in the Illinois Country.[22] Levadoux's arrival freed Gibault to accept the offer of the Spanish to become pastor at New Madrid.

From documentary evidence presently available it is impossible to determine exactly when Gibault took up residence at New Madrid during 1792. The single existing document relating to the point is a brief note, written to Gibault on July 16, 1792, from Thyrso Henrique Henriquez, assistant vicar-general of the bishop of Santiago de Cuba by which Father Gibault was directed to consult with Father de Saint Pierre concerning ecclesiastical problems.[23] The note seems to infer that de Saint Pierre was to be considered Gibault's local superior. In any case, it is clear that by July 1792 Pierre Gibault was considered to be the pastor at New Madrid and recognized as such by ecclesiastical authorities at New Orleans. Civil recognition of his appointment, essential for his receiving an annual salary from the state, was communicated to Gibault on June 5, 1793, by Ignacio Delino, military commandant for Spain at the Arkansas Post.[24]

Part of Father Gibault's responsibility at New Madrid was the spiritual care of the Arkansas Post, a small garrison village located on the left bank of the Arkansas River a few miles above that river's confluence with the Mississippi. The place had its beginning in 1686 when a few companions of Henry Tonty, La Salle's faithful lieutenant, procured permission to open a trading post there. The small center continued chiefly as a fort with a few families always in residence. Father Gibault visited there on September 15, 1792.[25] For a brief period during 1793 the Arkansas Post enjoyed the presence of a resident priest, Father Sebastien Flavien de Besancon, a Capuchin refugee from the French Revolution. In July 1793 Father Patrick Walsh, vicar-general of the bishop at New Orleans, wrote to Gibault: "I am granting you faculties so that on reaching New Madrid you may examine the Reverend Father Xavier, a Capuchin religious who is there, regarding his capacities and his faculties. Please send me information at the first opportunity so that I may know whether he is fitted for pastoral charge. This priest has orders to go to the Arkansas post to continue the work you began there, that is to preach and teach Christian Doctrine, but nothing else regarding the ministry, at least until we know the results of the information you forward."[26] Gibault's reply has not been preserved, but apparently it was none too favorable for the Capuchin was summoned to New Orleans in 1794 where he quite soon became involved in an unseemly altercation with some army officers for whose troops he acted as chaplain.[27] Thenceforth the Arkansas Post continued under Gibault's care. That he ministered there with great regularity is evident from the fact that, for example in a single year, September 1792 to September 1793, he baptized thirty persons at the Arkansas Post and witnessed twenty marriages.[28]

Pierre Gibault was barely settled at New Madrid before he found himself at odds with the ecclesiastical authority at New Orleans. After years on the frontier the old missionary probably considered himself at liberty to exercise jurisdiction which circumstances seemed to require. He was quickly pulled up short by a rather curt note from the vicar-general at New Orleans dated July 1793: "One of us seems to be mistaken regarding your faculties which I expressly granted you in my last letter. In it I said, or meant to say, that you could exercise your priestly functions without distinction of persons only in case of necessity and as far as granted by the Council of Trent to simple priests. These are the ones I granted you."[29] Possibly the vicar-general's letter was inspired by a complaint from Father de Saint Pierre, Gibault's immediate, local superior. Concerning de Saint Pierre, the vicar-general at New Orleans remarked in his letter to Gibault: "Meanwhile conditions favorable to you are developing because in a letter I received recently Father Paul de Saint Pierre, parish priest at Ste. Genevieve, is offering to give up his post there and he has already arranged the requisite details. And in his letter he wished me to tell you this."[30] One might infer from the above that if de Saint Pierre left Ste. Genevieve it was the intention of the authorities at New Orleans to appoint Father Gibault vicar-general for the area. However, Father de Saint Pierre remained at Ste. Genevieve until 1797 when he was succeeded by Father James Maxwell.[31]

After residing at New Madrid for perhaps eighteen months, Father Gibault took an irrevocable step, finally divorcing himself from his homeland as well as his original diocese. On December 23, 1793, the grizzled missionary took the oath of allegiance to the Spanish crown at Fort Celeste, near New Madrid, in the presence of the Spanish military commandant.[32] Father Gibault must have anticipated a tranquil future under the Spanish regime. He could expect an annual salary of $600 paid to him by the royal treasury.[33] To this would be added such donations as the faithful saw fit to contribute for his services. Tithing, a constant source of irritation between pastor and people under the French regime, as well as the system of *marguilliers* with its attendant petty squabbling, simply did not exist within the Spanish colony. Though the crown of Spain looked upon the

138

Church as a department of the civil state, at least the king supported the clergy financially, donated quite generously to building and repairing the churches, and backed the Church with civil authority in obliging the people to be at least outwardly faithful in the practice of their religion. Hence, the old apostolic warrior, Gibault, could relax, assured of adequate economic support as well as the strong arm of the law in maintaining the religious life of his people.

During the early years of its existence, New Madrid was not the isolated backwater community one would suppose it to have been. French refugees and some Americans, intriguing against the United States, drifted into the village. A small group of French nuns, members of a contemplative religious order, the Poor Clares, arrived sometime during 1793.[34] How they reached North America, how they ever came to New Madrid is an unsolved mystery. In 1794 the nuns moved on to New Orleans where they must have found temporary refuge with the Ursuline nuns there. New Madrid also became the American home of some of the disillusioned French who had been recruited and grossly deceived by the dishonest promoters of the Scioto Land Company. Seeking escape from the ravages of the French Revolution, a contingent of French purchased land on the little Scioto River in Ohio. On their arrival, the French learned that they had been bilked by the Scioto promoters who could not produce clear titles to the land the immigrants thought they had purchased. The French first settled at Gallipolis in 1791, but they soon drifted off, many settling at New Madrid.[35] Some of these French immigrants had renounced their Catholic faith in favor of deism and many others were very lax in their religious practices. Under Father Gibault's pastoral care many were brought back to their traditional religion. By 1798 the bishop of Louisiana took occasion to congratulate Gibault on his noteworthy success with that much abused group of suffering French immigrants.[36]

As the population of New Madrid increased with its hetero-geneous citizenry of French, Spanish, and Anglo-Saxon, together with their various religious backgrounds, Father Gibault sought direction from the vicar-general of New Orleans regarding his particular problems. On May 15, 1794, Father Patrick Walsh sent New Madrid's pastor a quite lengthy letter answering questions and, incidentally, highlighting the problems met by a frontier pastor.

Answering your letter of May 1, I must inform you that [the decrees of] the Council of Trent were promulgated in all Spanish domains and, consequently, must be observed in this whole province; and the Roman ritual is the one followed in this diocese. You must be aware of the distinction between a simple priest and a pastor. The latter can absolve all parishioners in all cases not reserved to the bishop, but a simple priest has no such jurisdiction because no part of the flock of Jesus Christ has yet been committed to his care. And, therefore, that you may be aware of the limits of your jurisdiction as pastor, they are as follows: you have no faculties, nor can I grant them (in my position as sub-delegate to the Ordinary) to dispense from the degrees of consanguinity, from affinity, public morality, spiritual relationship, nor the other direment impediments to marriage. As often as persons present themselves with these impediments to marriage, you must let me know, along with the reasons for asking dispensations.

As for dispensations from banns, the Ordinary charges me very particularly, in his instructions, not to grant the dispensation without very serious reasons. Therefore, he forbids it entirely to parish priests, except in cases where it is necessary to protect the honor of a family or of a woman, or if in danger of death someone wishes to marry in order to legitimize his child; or if he has been directed by his confessor to regularize his marriage with a woman with whom he has been living. In all of these cases one may presume the tacit consent of the Ordinary.

Pastors have faculties to bless the vestments and altar vessels of their churches, to absolve from heresy and reserved cases, to reconcile converts from Protestantism, and to bestow the plenary indulgence in the moment of death. All this [they may do] within the limits of their own parishes, carefully observing the instructions of the Roman ritual regarding absolving heretics, and requiring witnesses, in cases of reconciliation [to the Church], who will swear to it above their signatures, which [documents] will be kept in the parish archives.

This is what the Ordinary has instructed me to communicate to all pastors of the province. I enclose an *Ordo* so that you may know the feasts of obligation observed in the diocese.

Please examine the instructions sent by my predecessor for your guidance and that of all pastors. You will find in it a list of stipends about which you inquire.[37]

The year 1795 must have been an uneasy one for Pierre Gibault. In an effort to prevent its colony of Louisiana from being engulfed by Americans, especially those from Kentucky, Spanish officials, with the encouragement of the home government, had for years been carrying on an intrigue hoping to induce numbers of Americans to revolt against the United States in favor of Spain. In September 1795 Francisco Carondelet, governor of Louisiana, sent Manuel Gayoso de Lemos, commandant at Natchez, to New Madrid where he was expected to make final arrangements with the wily General James Wilkinson for the revolt. Playing both sides, Wilkinson delayed, temporized, and asked for more funds. Finally, in December, through his agent, Benjamin Sebastian, a meeting was arranged at New Orleans to be held early in January 1796. Reaching New Orleans at the designated time, the plotters were astounded to discover that on October 27, 1795, Spain and the United States had concluded the Treaty of San Lorenzo whereby Americans were granted free navigation of the Mississippi as well as the right to deposit their goods at New Orleans. Since the terms of the treaty eliminated the major complaints of western Americans, Wilkinson's whole plot fell of its own weight.[38]

No existing document indicates what Pierre Gibault might have thought of that swirl of activity taking place at his very doorstep. Only two letters addressed to him during that year have survived. The first, dated September 3, 1795, directed him to take a census of New Madrid, including the number of whites, half-breeds, free Negroes, and slaves with the ages and sex of each.[39] The second communication, November 16, 1795, informed Gibault that the war between France and Spain, begun in 1793, had been ended by the Treaty of Basel. Consequently each pastor was directed to celebrate a Mass of thanksgiving as well as the solemn chanting of the *Te Deum*.[40]

From 1795 forward Father Gibault was subject to the authority of Father James Maxwell, pastor of the parish of Ste. Genevieve and vicar-general of the upper reaches of Spanish Louisiana. Maxwell, born probably at Dublin in 1742, had done his ecclesiastical studies at the University of Salamanca. Together with several other Irish priests, he was recruited by the Spaniards in 1794 for the colony of Louisiana in the hope that they could convert English-speaking non-Catholics who settled in the colony.[41] Relations between Gibault and his newly appointed superior began unpropitiously and continued in much the same manner. On July 1, 1795, New Madrid's pastor received a letter from Bishop Peñalver sharply reminding Gibault that he no longer belonged to the diocese of Quebec, was no longer a vicar-general and must, therefore, obey the regulations of the diocese to which he now belonged.[42] Two years later, on May 31, 1797, Father Maxwell called Gibault to task for being too lenient.

> I received your letter of the 25 of this month, in which you ask my advice regarding several cases which have arisen in your parish. Regarding the first point you have not done enough. Monsieur Marche a Terre and that widow have given public scandal; they should be punished publicly and with severity. I am sure that the commandant will lend a hand to correct such abuses. Regarding the second point, I authorize you to marry François Michel and Catherine Bonneau without publication of banns, provided you are very sure no obstacle exists between them, except the lack of consent of the brother. In the four years of their past married life, about which you wrote, there existed only mutual consent,

but now you will add a sacrament, if they are Catholics. As to the third point, you will address yourself to the commandant to have that woman driven from Joseph Michel's house. If this is not done, you will let me know.[43]

If on reading that communication, Gibault controlled his temper, one could greatly admire him. Maxwell, who had been in the country barely two years, hardly needed to instruct a veteran missionary of thirty years on the principles of canon law. Besides, Maxwell's remark concerning the conferring of the sacrament of matrimony was erroneous theology.[44]

A second note from Maxwell, written on October 6, 1797, reveals some rather unpleasant facets of his character.

> I received your letter of September 5 in which you ask that Jean Baptiste Barjaloux be married without the publication of banns. You may allow it provided he pays 24 piastres, which you will remit to me at the first opportunity, provided, of course, that you are sure there is no impediment to the marriage. The fee for dispensations from the first two banns is 12 piastres, and for the third, 12 piastres. Thus you will conform to the regulations. The motives, which you allege, are not sufficient to allow the dispensation *gratis* for he can defer his marriage until he returns from the Nation, and then be married according to the prescribed laws. I hope you will not give me occasion to be displeased with you. . . . You ought to be instructed on all the regulations of the ministry, having been vicar-general yourself for such a long time in these regions, and you should, therefore, know the rights pertaining to that office.[45]

Pierre Gibault was, indeed, well aware of ecclesiastical regulations, to say nothing of the perquisites pertaining to the office of vicar-general. He also knew the needs of his people which Maxwell, in his profound inexperience, seems, not once, to have taken into consideration.

One incident of militant Catholicism which occurred during Gibault's tenure at New Madrid is worth recording, if only for its humorous value. In accord with the terms of the Treaty of San Lorenzo of 1795, surveying teams were sent to determine exactly where the newly delineated boundary of the United States lay. In June 1797 Andrew Elliott, the American commissioner for determining the new boundary, was at New Madrid, enjoying the hospitality of Manuel Gayoso de Lemos, Spanish commandant of upper Louisiana. A small group of American Baptists had settled nearby with their minister, Hannah. Elliott procured permission from Gayoso for Hannah to preach to the Americans in the surveying party, provided the minister refrained from discussing any political topics. Since the occasion was unique, the service, held on June 9, 1797, drew a large audience of the curious. A few days later the Reverend Hannah became involved in an unseemly altercation with a group of rough and ready Irish Catholics. Taking exception to some quite disparaging remarks Hannah made about Catholicism the Irish roundly thrashed him. Complaining to Gayoso, Hannah, a slightly built man, demanded justice, ". . . threatening at the same time to do it for himself, if his request was not complied with. The governor, with more patience and good temper than ordinary, advised him to reflect a few moments and then repeat his request, which the preacher did in the same words, accompanied with threats. Upon which the governor immediately ordered him to be committed to the prison, which was within the fort, and his legs to be placed in the stocks."[46]

Parenthetically, it might be remarked that, for his time, Pierre Gibault was surprisingly free of the current religious prejudices of his day, prejudices shared by Catholics and non-Catholics alike. Actually, on several occasions during his apostolic career Gibault received whole families into the Church. The last such documented occasion occurred at the Arkansas Post. On December 15, 1793, Jacob Darty, his wife, Anna Scheffer, and their six children, renouncing their Protestant faith, were all received into the Catholic faith.[47]

Just a month before the none too edifying incident occurred to the poor Baptist minister, Father Gibault was informed

144

by the bishop of Louisiana that the plans he had submitted for
a new church at New Madrid had been approved.[48] Since funds
for the building were supplied by the government, erection of
the structure was delayed until 1799 when the proper approval
was received from the civil authorities. Shortly thereafter, New
Madrid had a new church dedicated to St. Isidore as well as a
new rectory with an attached bakehouse.[49]

Almost by accident, a description of the church at New
Madrid and Father Gibault's rectory has survived. As a result
of Spain's retrocession of Louisiana to France in 1800, Spanish
officials in the colony were directed to have "the buildings belonging to the King [of Spain] inventoried and appraised by
experts. . . ."[50] The "experts" who performed that duty at New
Madrid on March 18, 1804, left the following description:

> Then we went immediately and first to the church with the
> experts who had been appointed, accompanied by witnesses. That
> building is sixty feet long, twenty-eight feet wide, and sixteen feet
> high between the ground and the ceiling. Its carpenter work is
> constructed of cypress timber doubled on the outside with planks
> of the same wood. It has a partition in its width for the sacristy,
> ten openings with their windows and gratings, an altar with a
> tabernacle of cherry wood, and a picture of the most holy Virgin
> Mary, eight feet high and five and a half feet wide, framed in
> wood, a railing in front where communion is taken, a pulpit of
> cherry wood, a belfry with a metal bell weighing fifty pounds.
> The experts estimate unanimously that it is altogether worth one
> thousand two hundred pesos.
>
> At the same time we went to the parish house. It is twenty-
> six feet long and sixteen feet wide, doubled without and within
> with cypress planks; the floor and ceiling, and a wall of cypress
> planks; a double brick chimney; four openings with their win-
> dows and doors and their gratings; a gallery in front, with a floor
> and ceiling; a cellar under said house, and a stairway to mount
> to a garret; another house which is used as a kitchen, and which
> is eighteen feet long and fifteen feet wide. The experts unani-
> mously agree that the whole is worth three hundred and fifty
> pesos.

At the same time we went with the experts and witnesses abovementioned to the bakehouse. That building is fifteen feet long and ten feet wide, and has a brick chimney, an oven thirty feet in circumference, with frames completely made of brick, with a roof made of carpenter work to cover it, a bread marker, a flour-sieve, shovels, pokers, casks, canvasses and sheets for covering the bread, and other utensils of little value. The experts unanimously estimated the whole at one hundred and twenty pesos.[51]

While the Spanish colonial officials seemed willing enough to furnish funds for erecting a church at New Madrid, they seemed quite unconcerned that the poor pastor's proper salary was not paid promptly. Having no other source of income, except the chance generosity of his people, Father Gibault, after receiving no funds between September 1797 and January 1799, finally sought remuneration. Juan Ventura Morales, the Spanish intendant at New Orleans informed the old pastor, on February 27, 1799, that if he wished to receive his salary he should grant power of attorney to some trustworthy agent residing at New Orleans. Funds were low, Gibault was informed, and only importuning authorities would get the desired results.[52] Whether people donated food for the pastor's table is unknown, but at least they didn't let him freeze. There has been preserved a schedule of wood delivered to Father Gibault at regular intervals from September 16, 1801, to January 5, 1802.[53]

As the years advanced, Pierre Gibault became, more and more, a thorn in the side of his immediate superior, Father James Maxwell. Apparently, with advancing age the old missionary grew more sympathetic toward people in trouble and less exacting in enforcing ecclesiastical regulations. Father Maxwell was particularly unhappy with the pastor of New Madrid for not insisting on contributions from the faithful when they were dispensed from such requirements as the publication of marriage banns. Such contributions belonged to the vicar-general, Maxwell. But on a frontier these rules could not be followed exactly. Those wishing to be married in the presence of

146

a priest often traveled great distances and could not remain any
lengthy period away from home. Nonetheless, Maxwell pressed
his point. In the last extant letter from him to Gibault, the vicar-
general was far from courteous to an old man. Strangely, Maxwell's letter smacks of so many which Gibault had received
during his arduous apostolic career.

On October 28, 1801, Maxwell wrote from Ste. Genevieve:

> Having learned that the inhabitants of Cape Girardeau who
> are non-Catholics go over to New Madrid to be joined in mar-
> riage by you, and that you received the consent of a man named
> Randall and Sara Staller, a minor, without the consent of her
> mother and brother, I warn you not to perform any more mar-
> riage ceremonies between persons of the said district, since it is
> in my jurisdiction. I have also heard that you give dispensations
> from banns right and left. You are enlightened enough to know
> that these powers and rights belong to me. Up to the present I
> have accorded you my protection and I have given a favorable
> answer to all questions which the bishop has asked regarding you,
> while telling me, at the same time, to keep a vigilant eye on your
> conduct. But I think that I shall find myself obliged to act quite
> differently if you do not give me some proof of your submission
> to the orders I give you.[54]

Shortly before the arrival of Maxwell's curt note, Pierre
Gibault received a kindly letter from Bishop Peñalver, advising
the pastor at New Madrid that Rome had appointed the bishop
to the post of archbishop of Guatemala. Informing Gibault that,
until a new bishop arrived, Father Thomas Hassett at New Orleans would have charge of the diocese, the departing prelate
continued:

> Although vigilance of the pastor of souls ought to be continuous,
> it is needful that it be redoubled during the absence of the first
> pastor of the diocese, lest the common enemy, making use of the
> opportunity, might attack that portion of the flock of Jesus Christ,
> scatter and devour it; for this reason I recommend it to you with
> confidence in your zeal that it will not happen here, and that the
> Supreme Judge may not have to demand of us an account of our

mission with severity. I place myself at your disposal as well as all your parish, whom I love in Jesus Christ and whom I bear in my heart. In my new destination and in whatever place [I may be] I would truthfully desire to please you. With this, I now ask God to preserve you for many years.[55]

Perhaps this was only a form letter sent to every pastor within the diocese. But for once, at least, a bishop spoke kindly to Pierre Gibault.

Pierre Gibault was not destined to be granted the many years which the bishop wished for him. On August 16, 1802, at about seven in the morning, Gibault died in his rectory at New Madrid.[56] The sacristan of the parish, Louis Baby, notified Henri Peyroux, Spanish commandant of New Madrid, of the priest's death. That very day, Peyroux, accompanied by Pierre Lasorco and Baby, went to the church and made an inventory of Gibault's personal property found there. The following day, the deceased priest's effects found in the rectory were inventoried and later sold at auction.[57] There is no extant account of the priest's burial, but it is supposed that his wasted body was laid to rest within the church of St. Isidore. One would hope that Father James Maxwell was informed and had the courtesy to come to New Madrid to preside over the obsequies of the old apostle who, for thirty-four years, kept the light of Christianity alive in the Mississippi Valley.

Erosion caused by the mighty Mississippi plus the disastrous New Madrid earthquake of December 16, 1811, has long since removed all evidence of the New Madrid with which Pierre Gibault was familiar. Even the patron of the parish there has been changed from St. Isidore to the Immaculate Conception. No noteworthy monument at New Madrid reminds the visitor that the Patriot Priest established Catholicity there. But neither Ste. Genevieve nor Vincennes have forgotten him. Each has raised a monument in his honor. For Pierre Gibault, it is perhaps honor enough to have served God well against constant

148

misunderstanding. It may well be that when Benjamin Franklin worked out the details of our treaty with England in that impressive palace overlooking the Place de la Concorde at Paris he was unaware of our claim to the east bank of the Mississippi River. However, it remains forever true that the devotion of Pierre Gibault went far to make George Rogers Clark's invasion of the West an eminent success. Not all America's heroes have received their due praise. As our country approaches the celebration of the second century since the opening of the American Revolution, it is proper to recall that an important figure in that epochal effort was a simple priest with vision.

# FATHER GIBAULT'S LIBRARY

On August 17, 1802, the day after Father Gibault's death, Louis Baby, sacristan of the parish, Henri Peyroux, Spanish commandant at New Madrid, and a few others inventoried the contents of Father Gibault's rectory. Among the effects discovered were 243 books which were listed by lot. On April 3, 1803, Father Gibault's effects were sold at public auction. Joseph Michel, a local merchant, purchased 211 of the deceased priest's books which were listed as follows:[1]

> Three dictionaries: one French and Latin,
>    one Latin and French, and a third Latin
>    and English                          1 piastre, 1 real.
> Five volumes on the rudiments of Lat[in]         4

151

| | | |
|---|---|---|
| Ovid, Cicero, Juvenal in five volumes | | 4 real. |
| Four volumes on surgery, medicine, and botany | 4 piastre, | |
| Ten volumes on diverse subjects | | 4 |
| Four volumes on cooking, agriculture, and fine arts | 2 | |
| Sixteen volumes of the Journal of Sav [?][2] | 3 | 2 |
| Two books of plain chant, two of hymns, and one of the canticles | 1 | |
| Breviaries for summer and winter, two volumes | | 4 |
| Roman breviary [complete] in two volumes in quarto | 2 | 5 |
| Four volumes of meditations by Beuvelet, Hayneuf, and Rodriquez[3] | 1 | |
| Concordance of the Bible and commentaries on the psalms of David, two volumes in quarto | 1 | |
| Theological conferences and dissertations of Calmet, three volumes in quarto[4] | 6 | 4 |
| Commentary on the Holy Scripture, one volume in folio | 1 | |
| Cases of conscience by Lamette and Fromageau, two volumes in folio[5] | 3 | |
| Cases of conscience by Pontas, three volumes in folio[6] | 5 | 4 |
| Four volumes of meditations by Hayneuf and another volume on the same subject, in all five volumes[7] | 1 | 2 |
| Collection Theologique, seven volumes in duodecimo | 1 | 4 |
| Moral theology, six volumes in duodecimo | 1 | 5 |
| Christian meditations, five volumes | 1 | 2 |
| Mission sermons, six volumes | | 6 |
| Sermons by Giroulet, Joly, and La Cheminaye, six volumes[8] | | 6 |
| Sermons by diverse persons, five volumes | 1 | 2 |
| Nine volumes by Massillon[9] | 1 | 5 |
| Eight volumes by Bourdaloue[10] | 1 | 2 |

152

| | |
|---|---|
| Five volumes, Epistles, Gospels, and Christian meditations | 4 real. |
| Six volumes on prayer and repentance | 4 |
| Five volumes, including the Bible and other works on prayer | 4 |
| Eight volumes on the Councils and the Fathers of the Church | 6 piastre, 4 |
| Conferences of Ange[r?], twenty-four volumes[11] | 4 |
| Thirty-five volumes on ecclesiastical history[12] | 20 |

---

# AN UNPUBLISHED LETTER OF

# JEAN-OLIVIER BRIAND,

# BISHOP OF QUEBEC,

# TO FATHER PIERRE GIBAULT,

# MAY 15, 1768

Jean-Olivier Briand, Bishop of Quebec

To our dearly-beloved son in our Lord, Pierre Gibault, priest, destined for the missions of the Illinois, greetings and benediction.[1]

Our Master, sending his apostles to preach the Gospel instructed them to conduct themselves with the wisdom of the serpent and the simplicity of the dove, warning them that he was sending them into the midst of wolves and that they should show themselves as lambs. *"Ecce, mitto vos sicut oves in medio luporum. Estote, ergo, prudentes sicut serpentes et simplices sicut columbae."*[2] There, our very dear son in our Lord, is, in a few words, the instruction which we feel ourselves obliged to give you. Be [like unto] a lamb so that the wolves to whom I send you, as I have been sent by Christ Jesus, may become lambs.[3] Remember always that people never become Christians through violence, but by persuasion. "For of his own will hath he begotten us by the word of

154

truth. . . ."[4] If the apostles had been lions, they would not have converted the world, nor conquered the wolves which populated it. But, because they had the gentleness of lambs, they drew men to become disciples of Christ like themselves. Never depart from that example. I do not mean to infer that it is necessary to be unduly soft and indulgent. ". . . reprove, entreat, rebuke . . ." says the apostle, inspired with the spirit of our Lord.[5] But severity ought to proceed only from afar, after kindness and Christian patience is exhausted [illegible]. ". . . in all patience . . . ," adds the same apostle.[6] Recall the forbearance and patience of our Lord with his apostles. Three years, passed in instruction and example, did not suffice to render them firm and constant in virtue. The chief fell and denied [our Lord]; the others fled, abandoning him on the critical occasion. I do not know if our Lord's resurrection put the apostles above human frailty. Scripture is silent on that matter and we could hold without temerity that our Lord ascended into heaven with having the consolation of seeing them perfect. In the opinion of the Church, they were so only after the descent of the Holy Spirit. Let us not, therefore, act too precipitantly or be angry if a person is not converted at the first, nor the second nor the hundredth instruction or reproof. But continue with patience, if not for the sake of the sinner, at least for yourself. Thus you will always derive fruit from your work. Persevere in order that you may not render yourself guilty. If the sinner perishes without your having warned him, you will perish with him as God tells us in Isaias.[7] To instruction, join prayer [illegible]. If St. Stephen had not prayed for St. Paul, would he have become a vessel of election? Would the Church have been enriched by his precious epistles? With a mother less saintly, what would St. Augustine have become? All fervent missionaries have been men of prayer. Without it, all of our efforts are powerless because, without the help of God and his grace, we can do nothing. ". . . neither he that planteth is anything, nor he that watereth; but God that giveth the increase."[8] Another reason, which concerns you personally, is that without prayer you will not persevere. You will soon become insipid salt, a mediator more fitted to alienate God, to excite his anger than to appease him. Do not lose sight of these truths which are already known to you. Often call them to mind.

Take good care to familiarize yourself with holy things. Always treat the sacraments with respect. Avoid all precipitation, especially in the tremendous mystery of the altar. From time to time, review in your mind your rubrics so that you never deviate from them. The ceremonies aid devotion. Be on your guard against routine which extinguishes faith and destroys piety.

Avoid showing preference for anyone and have no favorite families. As much as possible, do not be served by persons of the opposite sex, unless they be of advanced age and of irreproachable morals. I would prefer that you had none of them at all because there is no one more suspicious than the religiously indifferent. And, as you know, in that area almost everyone is that. Besides, you must be an excellent example, as the first sent by me, on whom those I will eventually send will pattern themselves.

Receive everyone politely and without arrogance. Take care, however, not to be too communicative. Speak politely, even to the poorest and humblest. Avoid pestering; rather put up with things. God will have his day. Keep yourself in union with the commandant and English officers. Dine rarely with them and avoid following them into excesses, if they fall into them at times.

Where religious principles permit you to give way, do not remain inflexible. Thereby you sustain the essentials. If something happens against good order, write about it to the general and to me.[9] While awaiting an answer, remain tranquil; God does not ask the impossible of us. Live in holy union with Père Meurin and all the missionaries who will be in the district. Study how to show yourself a minister [illegible] and irreprehensible in all things. Although you ought not to be interested at all in amassing money, do not yield in the matter of fees and stipends. Since the priest must live by the altar, it would be impossible to keep missionaries there if they lacked the necessities of life. ". . . they who serve the altar, partake with the altar," and ". . . the laborer is worthy of his hire."[10]

As it is necessary to follow a uniform and constant rule, you will be permitted to establish a schedule of fees and stipends, having regard to the abilities of the people and the cost of things necessary and useful to the missionaries. Send it to me, supported by proof, and I will approve it. Put all the missionaries under the obligation of following it. Nothing is more contrary to good order than when some require and others give way. The latter ordinarily seek their own interest. Although they might pretend to act out of disinterestedness, they always act against prudence and would seem to accuse others of self-interest.

Do not permit the missionaries to engage in commerce and have no dealings with it yourself, except regarding the tithes and [illegible] to the salary given you. Avoid all communication with those foreign to the state. Discourage the people from harboring a visionary hope of the return of the French. On the contrary, incline them to great docility toward the [British] commandant and an attachment to the [present] government. This is [in accord with] the spirit of our holy religion. On it depends peace and tranquillity as well as the liberty to practice our holy religion. You must inspire the savages with the same spirit, either yourself, if you have occasion, or through the missionaries sent to them. Exhort the people to engage in agriculture. This will render them sedentary and put them to work. Idleness and wandering are the causes of the disorders of the peoples of those districts.

Encourage youth to marry early. This is the means of hindering dissolute living. If possible, issue some regulations requiring married people to sleep [together] in separate apartments.

Do not allow anyone to attend Mass indecently attired. If this happens, request them to leave or do not celebrate the Mass. Inform them that I have forbidden you. Instruct the other missionaries that such is my intention.

Do not exercise rigidly the authority I give you for granting marriage dispensations, supposing that it is rare in a country so sparsely populated many families would not be related by blood or marriage. The [illegible, stipend?] in Canada for one bond is 12 [livres?], about 24 for two, about 96 for three, about 42 from the 4th to the 3rd, about 48 for the 3rd and from the 2nd to the 3rd in proportion.[11] The faculties sometimes fifty crowns, sometimes 100 crowns. And sometimes a hundred pounds only. Spiritual relationship is about 24. One does not require anything for the occult impediments. Notice that you may dispense from all the impediments to marriage which may arise unexpectedly *quantum ad petendum et reddendum debitum, et ad rehabilitationem matrimonii jam contracti quodque in confessione* [illegible] *invalidum fuisse propter impedimentum dirimens celebrationem matrimonii procedens.*[12] [Illegible] you can increase or decrease according to the abundance or scarcity of ready money in thos  areas. You will use the proceeds from dispensations for the poor the churches or [illegible] even for yourself if your revenue does not suffice; yet with discretion. Ordinarily, to avoid murmuring, the rich and poor are to be charged the same amount. It is only with those who are extremely poor that you can and should reduce, or even dispense gratis, imposing prayers or other good works, according to circumstances.

This is the advice which I thought to give you for your own conduct and that of others. If I had more time, I would have arranged it better and, perhaps, other ideas would have occurred to me. I hope that you will render an account, later, of what will be proper to regulate. May God keep you in his holy grace and direct your steps. Amen.

Jean-Olivier, Bishop of Quebec.
May 15, 1768

# NOTES

---

The following abbreviations were used in the notes.

AAQ—Archives of the Archdiocese of Quebec

IHC—*Illinois State Historical Society Collections*

NMA—New Madrid Archives

RACH—*Records of the American Catholic Historical Society of Philadelphia*

*Relations—The Jesuit Relations and Allied Documents*

## CHAPTER II

1 Clarence Walworth Alvord, *The Illinois Country 1673-1818* (Chicago: Loyola University Press, 1965), p. 170. He is quoting a letter of Bienville to the minister, July 25, 1733. The letter is found in Archives Nationales, Colonies, B, 16:265 ff.

2 During the colonial period the French knew almost nothing about the Rocky Mountains, but they claimed all of the land west of the Mississippi.

3 The French can be said to have had somewhat effective control of the area now contained within the borders of the states of Illinois, Indiana, and a bare fringe of eastern Missouri.

4 For a brief discussion of the ancient Hopewell civilization of the area, see Robert Silverberg, ". . . and the mound builders vanished from the earth," *American Heritage* XX (1969), 60-63, 90-95. For an extensive study of the subject, consult his recently published *Mound Builders of Ancient America* (New York: Graphic Arts, 1968). Monks Mound measures 998 by 721 feet at the base and covers 16 acres. It is estimated that the mound contains 21,600,000 cubic feet of earth. By comparison, the Bent Pyramid at Dashur on the Nile, not 20 miles south of Cairo, has a base of 188.6 meters square and is 101.15 meters high. See Ahmed Fakhry, *The Pyramids* (Chicago: University of Chicago Press, 1961), p. 88.

5 A relative of the famous Henry Tonty, Pierre de Liette, who spent forty years among the Indians in the Illinois Country, described the physical appearance of these aborigines thus: "You can see no finer looking people. Usually they are neither tall nor short; there are some you could encompass with your two hands. They have legs that seem drawn with an artist's pen. They carry their load of wood gracefully, with a proud gait, as finely as the best dancer. They have faces as beautiful as white milk, in so far as this is possible for Indians of that country. They have the most regular and whitest teeth imaginable. They are full of life, yet at the same time lazy." See Milo M. Quaife, editor, *The Western Country in the 17th Century* (Chicago: Lakeside Press, 1947), p. 111.

6 See Marquette's description of the Kaskaskia village he visited with Jolliet in 1673 in Reuben G. Thwaites, editor, *The Jesuit Relations and Allied Documents* (Cleveland: Burrows, 1896-1901), LIX, 127, 129. This source is henceforth cited as *Relations*.

7 Ibid., LI, 49. Allouez was wrong about his conclusion as later and more accurate observations by Marquette would attest.

8 Ibid., LIX, 165.

9 In 1679, La Salle built a fort at the mouth of the St. Joseph River near the site of the present St. Joseph, Michigan. In January 1680 he erected Fort Crèvecoeur at the southern end of Peoria Lake near the present Peoria, Illinois. On his way back from locating the mouth of the Mississippi, in 1682, he built Fort Prud'homme at the Chickasaw Bluffs. In December of that same year he established Fort St. Louis on the scant acre of land atop Starved Rock in the Illinois River near Utica, Illinois. He also erected a small stockade at the Chicago portage, a location now within the city of Chicago. None of these forts was permanent.

10 The account of his visit may be consulted in *Relations*, LX, 149-67.

11 Ibid.

12 Ibid., LXV, 264. From 1691 to 1693 Gravier was assisted by Father Sebastien Rale who was later sent to administer to the Abenaki in Maine where he was murdered by the English at his mission near Norridgewock, Maine, on August 23, 1724.

13 Ibid., LXIV, 159, 161. The fort itself was moved during the winter of 1691-1692. Gravier did not migrate to the new site until the spring of 1693.

14 Ibid., LXVI, 253.

15 Ibid., LXV, 53-57.

16  Ibid., 103.

17  H. Têtu and C. O. Gagnon, editors, *Mandements, lettres pastorales et circulaires des évêques de Québec* (Quebec: The editors, 1887-1890), I, 274-370, 377. The mission requested by the group was not their first such effort. One of their missionaries, Father Louis Pierre Thury, established a mission in Acadia in 1684. See Bishop Jean-Baptiste Saint-Vallier, *Estat présent de l'eglise et de la colonie française dans la Nouvelle-France* (Paris: Coté, 1856), pp. 45-52.

18  J. H. Schlarman, *From Quebec to New Orleans* (Belleville, Ill.: Buechler, 1929), pp. 130-47. See also Joseph P. Donnelly, *The Parish of the Holy Family, Cahokia, Illinois, 1699-1949* (Cahokia, Ill.: 250th Anniversary Association, 1949).

19  John G. Shea, *The Catholic Church in Colonial Days* (New York: The author, 1886), pp. 541-44. Fortunately the controversy did not prevent all missionaries actually in the field from treating one another with singular charity.

20  Alvord, *Illinois Country*, p. 145.

21  Quaife, *Western Country*, pp. 77-78.

22  Emile Laurière, *Histoire de la Louisiane française, 1673-1939* (Paris: Maisonneuve, 1940), pp. 319-24.

23  Alvord, *Illinois Country*, p. 203.

24  For a study of French law during the period, see Ernest Glasson, *Précis elémentaire de l'histoire du droit français* (Paris: Chaumont, 1874).

25  Alvord, *Illinois Country*, pp. 194-95.

26  Joseph P. Donnelly, *Jacques Marquette, S.J., 1637-1675* (Chicago: Loyola University Press, 1968), p. 246. See also *Relations*, LIX, 177. At least two such traders spent the winter, 1674-1675, in the neighborhood of the Chicago portage where Marquette lay ill. One was Pierre Moreau who had accompanied Jolliet and Marquette on their voyage down the Mississippi in 1673. The other is known only as the surgeon.

27  In 1679, fourteen men accompanied La Salle. On his expedition in 1680 twenty-five men were with him. In 1682 he had twenty-three men in his party.

28  Alvord, *Illinois Country*, p. 156.

29  Gregory M. Franzwa, *The Story of Old Ste. Genevieve* (St. Louis: Patrice Press, 1967), p. 20.

30  *Relations*, LXX, 316.

31  Ibid., 233. Strangely, the church was dedicated to St. Joachim, not Ste. Genevieve.

32  Ibid., 316.

33  Alvord, *Illinois Country*, p. 202.

34  Natalia M. Belting, *Kaskaskia under the French Regime* (Urbana: University of Illinois Press, 1948), p. 39.

35  Clarence W. Alvord and Clarence E. Carter, editors, *The New Régime, 1765-1767, Illinois State Historical Society Collections* XI, *British Series* II (Springfield: Illinois State Historical Library, 1916), 469. This source is henceforth cited as IHC, XI.

36  N. M. Surrey, *The Commerce of Louisiana during the French Régime, 1699-1763* (New York: Longmans, 1916), pp. 289, 300-01.

37  Ibid., p. 299.
38  Belting, *Kaskaskia*, pp. 61-63.


CHAPTER III

1   Jean Delanglez, *The French Jesuits in Lower Louisiana (1700-1763)* (Washington, D. C.: Catholic University Press, 1935), pp. 499-500. Nicolas Chauvin de la Frénière was a native of New Orleans, having been born there on September 30, 1728. Educated in France, he returned to Louisiana in 1748 when he was about twenty. In 1752 he went to France on business and remained there three years, during which time he was admitted to the bar. As an *avocat en Parlement,* he was probably prejudiced against the Jesuits, but as an official of the colony he conducted himself quite properly.

2   Ibid., p. 522. Delanglez characterizes Laissard thus: ". . . the Substitute Attorney was one of those zealous individuals whose ideas of justice were rather rudimentary, and who thought that the decree was not sufficiently odious, but that, for good measure, he had to add some of his churlishness in executing it."

3   *Relations,* LXX, 269.

4   Delanglez, *French Jesuits,* p. 509.

5   Ibid.

6   The one dissenting vote was cast by ". . . M. de Châtillon, lieutenant-general of the regiment of Angoumois . . . This worthy old man did not fear to declare himself for those to whom so little protection then remained." *Relations,* LXX, 219.

7   Delanglez, *French Jesuits,* pp. 511-12.

8   The European Jesuit college of the eighteenth century was not the exact equivalent of a college for undergraduates in the United States today. A student enrolled at the Jesuit college as young as twelve and remained until he was about eighteen.

9   A few noted Jesuit scientists were Christopher Clavius, the father of our Gregorian calendar; Paul Guldin, discoverer of Guldin's Rule; Christopher Scheiner, who first observed sunspots and refraction of the atmosphere; Roger Boscovich, who invented the ring micrometer; Athanasius Kircher, who was called the Doctor of a Hundred Arts.

10  The Jesuits were exiled from Portugal on January 13, 1759; from France on August 6, 1762; and from Spain on February 27, 1767.

11  Even d'Alembert, leader of the French Encyclopedists, recognized the protection the Jesuits rendered the papacy. He wrote to Frederick the Great of Prussia: "It would be madness for the Pope to destroy his bodyguard to please the Catholic princes . . ." See Martin P. Harney, *The Jesuits in History* (New York: America Press, 1941), p. 292.

12  Jacques Crétineau-Joly, *Histoire religieuse, politique et littéraire de la Compagnie de Jésus* (Paris: Poussielgue-Rusand, 1854), V, 190.

13  Ibid., 195-96.

14  Ibid., 226.

15 Delanglez, *French Jesuits*, p. 505.

16 Ibid., p. 506.

17 Marc de Villiers de Terrage, *Les dernières années de la Louisiane française* (Paris: Guilmoto, 1904), p. 154.

18 In 1763 there were twelve Jesuit priests in the colony of Louisiana. In the New Orleans area were Michel Baudouin, the superior, aged seventy-two, a native Canadian; Louis Carette, fifty-one, missionary at the Arkansas Post until his recall to New Orleans in 1758; Nicolas Le Febvre, forty-eight; Jean Le Prédour, forty-one, missionary at Fort Toulouse; and Maximilien Le Roy, aged forty-seven. In the Illinois Country were Philippe Watrin, superior of that local mission, aged sixty-six; Jean Aubert, forty-one, curé of the French who lived at the village of Kaskaskia; Julien De Verney, fifty-four, missionary at Vincennes; Jean La Morinie, forty-eight; Sebastien Meurin, fifty-six; Pierre Potier, fifty-five; and Jean Salleneuve, fifty-five. The last two were at Kaskaskia by accident, having recently fled from Detroit to escape the English forces.

19 Ironically, before these Jesuits left New Orleans they were given a letter addressed to the primary author of their disaster, Choiseul, commending them to his charity. See *Relations*, LXX, 291, 301.

20 Ibid., 291.

21 Ibid., 293.

22 Camille de Rochemonteix, *Les Jésuites de la Nouvelle-France au XVIIIe siècle* (Paris: Picard, 1906), I, 391.

23 IHC, XI, 522. Meurin to Briand, March 23, 1767.

24 *Relations*, LXX, 315.

25 IHC, XI, 527. Meurin to Briand, March 23, 1767.

26 Ibid., 527-28.

27 Ibid., 527.

28 Charles H. Metzger, "Sebastien Louis Meurin, S.J.," *Illinois Catholic Historical Review* III (1920-1921), 372.

29 IHC, XI, 522. Meurin to Briand, March 23, 1767.

30 Ibid., 523.

31 Ibid., 589-91. Briand to the Kaskaskians, August 7, 1767.

32 Ibid.

33 Thomas A. Hughes, *The History of the Society of Jesus in North America* (New York: Longmans, 1908-1917), Text II, 598.

34 IHC, XI, 529. Meurin to Briand, March 23, 1767. Jean Mercier, a priest of the society of the Missions-Etrangères, labored as a missionary at Cahokia from 1718 to 1753. He had been appointed vicar-general by the bishop of Quebec for the area in which he worked. Laurent and Forget, members of the same society, succeeded Mercier at Cahokia, and with the same ecclesiastical authority. Actually Father Meurin had no objective cause for concern regarding his own faculties. He had been granted jurisdiction years before by his own superior who was fully empowered to do so. The suppression of the Society of Jesus by the French civil authorities in no way affected Meurin's ecclesiastical faculties which could be revoked only by the bishop who had granted them or by the Holy See. Neither had done so.

35  Ibid., 558-65. Briand to Meurin, April 28 [?], 1767.

36  Schlarman, *Quebec to New Orleans*, p. 443.

37 ' *Relations*, LXXI, 35.

38  Schlarman, *Quebec to New Orleans*, p. 365.

39  Clarence W. Alvord and Clarence E. Carter, editors, *Trade and Politics, 1767-1769, Illinois State Historical Society Collections* XVI, *British Series* III (Springfield: Illinois State Historical Library, 1921), 304-05. This source is henceforth cited as IHC, XVI.

40  Ibid.

41  Ibid.

42  Gilbert J. Garraghan, *The Jesuits of the Middle United States* (New York: America Press, 1938), I, 8, gives the date of Meurin's death as February 23, 1777. Schlarman, *Quebec to New Orleans*, p. 444, says that Meurin died on August 12, 1777. The date given by Garraghan is correct.


CHAPTER IV

1  Cyprien Tanguay, *Dictionnaire généalogique des familles canadiennes depuis la fondation de la colonie jusqu'à nos jours* (Montreal: Senécal, 1871-1880), IV, 261. In New France, Gabriel was known as Gibault *dit* Poitevin or "from Poitiers," much as in English one might say "Smith, the Texan."

2  Louis Fleureau, "La famille Margane de Lavaltrie," *Bulletin des Recherches Historiques* XXIII (1917), 35.

.3  Tanguay, *Dictionnaire généalogique*, IV, 262.

4  The Missouri Historical Society (St. Louis) possesses a copy of Gibault's will. The original document appears to have been lost. In the society's archives the copy is identified as New Madrid Archives, XI, 1431. This documentary source is henceforth cited at NMA.

5  Raymond Douville and Jacques-Donat Casanova, *Daily Life in Early Canada* (New York: Macmillan, 1968), p. 204.

6  Amédée Gosselin, *L'Instruction au Canada sous le régime français (1635-1760)* (Quebec: Laflamme, 1911), p. 133. Gosselin includes the quote from Peter Kalm.

7  See John F. McDermott, "The Library of Father Gibault," *Mid-America* XVII (1935), 273-75.

8  *Records of the American Catholic Historical Society of Philadelphia*, XX (1909), 423-24. Gibault to Briand, December 4, 1775. This source is henceforth cited as RACH.

9  IHC, XVI, 537. Briand to Gibault, April 26, 1769. In his *L'Eglise du Canada après la conquête* (Quebec: Laflamme, 1916-1917), II, 330, Auguste Gosselin says that Gibault was taken to the Illinois Country by his parents when Pierre was quite young and brought back by them after a few years. Gosselin's authority for his statement is a letter Briand wrote to Gibault on April 26, 1769. Briand merely said: "Even though you knew the country as it was previously, I warned you that it had changed."

10  IHC, XVI, 611. Gibault to Briand, October [?], 1769.

11  Ibid., 421. Resolves of the Seminary of Quebec, October 11, 1768. ". . . It is just that this mission . . . shall now of itself provide missionary priests . . . and also share in the expenses of the education of M. Gibault, priest, who has just been sent thither and whose entire education was charged to the Seminary."

12  Gosselin, *L'Eglise du Canada*, II, 330-31.

13  Tanguay, *Dictionnaire généalogique*, IV, 262.

14  Gosselin, *L'Eglise du Canada*, II, 331. See also IHC, XVI, 535. Briand to Meurin, April 26, 1769.

15  Briand to Gibault, May 15, 1768. This unpublished letter is in the archives of Notre Dame University, Notre Dame, Indiana.

16  IHC, XVI, 295, 297. Briand to Gibault, May 30, 1768.

17  Ibid., 306. Meurin to Briand, June 11, 1768.

18  Douville and Casanova, *Early Canada*, p. 188.

19  *Wisconsin Historical Collections* XVIII (1908), 292-93. In this source the license is dated June 1, but the original in the Chicago Historical Society gives the date as June 7.

20  IHC, XVI, 618-19. Gibault to Briand, October [?], 1769.

21  Ibid.

22  Ibid., XI, 528. Meurin to Briand, March 23, 1767.

23  Gosselin, *L'Eglise du Canada*, II, 331.

24  *Tripe de roche* is an edible species of lichen. Though completely tasteless, it will sustain life.

25  Major Robert Rogers of Rogers' Rangers fame had only recently been relieved of his command at Fort Michilimackinac. He was shipped off in irons to Montreal where he stood trial for treason. Acquitted, he went to London where he was thrown into debtor's prison.

26  This was Father Pierre Du Jaunay, the last Jesuit missionary to serve the Michilimackinac area. He departed in 1765 and died at Quebec in 1780.

27  Archives of the Archdiocese of Quebec, E.U., VI, 10. Gibault to Briand, July 28, 1768. This archival source is hereafter referred to as AAQ.

28  *Wisconsin Historical Collections* XVIII (1908), 487-88. Gibault should not have said that he validated the marriage nor should he have said that the ceremony legitimized the child. During the protracted absence of a priest, two Catholics may validly marry before witnesses just as this couple had done. The marriage was perfectly valid and the child was legitimate.

29  IHC, XVI, 536. Briand to Gibault, April 26, 1769.

30  George Pare and Milo M. Quaife, editors, "The St. Joseph Baptismal Register," *Mississippi Valley Historical Review* XIII (1926-1927), 235-36.

31  IHC, XVI, 501. Gibault to Briand, February 15, 1769.

32  Ibid.

33  Ibid., 549. Meurin to Briand, June 14, 1769. At the time people thought that the fever was caused by a poisonous miasma arising from the prairie sod in the late summer and fall. The true cause was probably malaria transmitted by swarms of mosquitoes as well as lack of sanitation. Gibault was not completely rid of the fever until 1770.

CHAPTER V

1   IHC, XVI, 553. Meurin to Briand, June 14, 1769.

2   Ibid., 550-51.

3   Ibid., 549.

4   Ibid., 502-03. Gibault to Briand, February 15, 1769.

5   Ibid., 581. Briand to Gibault, August 13, 1769.

6   Ibid., 304-05. Meurin to Briand, June 11, 1768. See also ibid., XI, 524-25, Meurin to Briand, March 23, 1767, relating a similar fate to the church of St. Anne at Fort Chartres.

7   John Francis McDermott, editor, *Old Cahokia: A Narrative and Documents Illustrating the First Century of Its History* (St. Louis: Historical Documents Foundation, 1949), illustration facing p. 16. This is an enlargement of the plan of the landholding of the mission drawn in 1735. See likewise Joseph P. Donnelly, editor, "The Founding of the Holy Family Mission," in McDermott, *Old Cahokia*, pp. 75-78, Father Jean Baptiste Mercier's explanation of the plan of the mission.

8   Ibid., pp. 81-83. Bill of sale of the mission on November 5, 1763.

9   IHC, XI, 565-67. Boiret to Meurin, May 3, 1767. See also ibid., XVI, 302-05, 311-14, Meurin to Boiret, June 11, 1768.

10   Ibid., 302-03. Meurin to Briand, June 11, 1768.

11   Ibid., 614-15. Gibault to Briand, March [?], 1770. A copy of the letter granting Gibault power of attorney may be examined in AAQ, E.U., VI, 55.

12   IHC, XVI, 503. Gibault to Briand, February 15, 1769.

13   The original records of baptisms and marriages of the parish of the Immaculate Conception at Kaskaskia, covering the period 1741 to 1834, are on deposit at St. Louis University, St. Louis, Missouri. Material offered here is gleaned from those records.

14   The names of these children were Marie Louise, baptized August 13, 1771; Marie Joseph, January 1, 1773; Joseph Pierre, February 27, 1774; and Marie Fortunee, May 22, 1778.

15   IHC, XVI, 560. Gibault to Briand, June 15, 1769.

16   Colton Storm, "The Notorious Colonel Wilkins," *Illinois State Historical Society Journal* XL (1947), 11.

17   The burial records made by Gibault are clearly not complete. Several pages are half blank and many entries are not in chronological order.

18   IHC, XI, 124-25. Sterling to Gage, December 15, 1765. ". . . this priest [Meurin] might be of great use to us, if he was brought over to this side, which I make no doubt might be effectuated, provided his former appointments were allowed him, which was 600 livres pr. Annum from the King as priest to the Indians."

19   Ibid., XVI, 623. Gibault to Briand, March [?], 1770. "As for me, no one has failed to pay me the tithes anywhere, and yet I never said a word about it. Poor and rich, good and bad, nobody has been so much in arrears that I had to ask for them."

20 Fintan G. Walker, "Some Correspondence of an Eighteenth Century Bishop with His Missionaries, 1767-1778," *Catholic Historical Review* XXVII (1941-1942), 189-90. Briand to Gibault, March 22, 1770, and August 16, 1770.

21 Edmund Flagg, who visited Kaskaskia in 1836, just two years before the structure was torn down, described the church as ". . . a huge old pile . . . its walls of hewn timbers perpendicularly planted and the interstices stuffed with mortar . . . the interior . . . is somewhat imposing notwithstanding the somber hue of its walls which are rudely plastered with lime and decorated with a few dingy paintings." Edmund Flagg, "The Far West," in Reuben G. Thwaites, editor, *Early Western Travels* (Cleveland: Clark, 1906), XXVII, 62-63.

22 IHC, XVI, 502. Gibault to Briand, February 15, 1769.

23 Ste. Genevieve, Missouri, Ste. Genevieve parish records. The entry appears on p. 51 of the bound volume entitled "Liber Baptismorum Parochiae Stae. Genovefae ab Anno 1760 ad Annum 1786."

24 IHC, XI, 555-56. Phillibert to Briand, April 6, 1767.

25 Ibid., XVI, 522-23. Ste. Marie et al. to Briand, April 22, 1769. The letter is signed first by Ste. Marie, Commandant. This man's real name was Jean Baptiste Racine. See Jacob P. Dunn, "Father Gibault: The Patriot Priest of the Northwest," *Illinois Historical Society Transactions*, 1905, p. 20.

26 IHC, XVI, 611. Gibault to Briand, March [?], 1770. In this same communication (621-22), Gibault informed the bishop: "I want to inform you that when I go on a journey I am always armed with my gun and two pistols, with the intention of preventing my being attacked. . . ." Two years later he gave up that practice. See below, note 30.

27 Ibid., 612.

28 Ibid., 611.

29 Vincennes, Indiana, Old Cathedral Archives: Parish of St. Francis Xavier, parish records, 1770-1831. Gibault was at Vincennes in February 1771, January 1773, February 1775, and June 1777.

30 AAQ, E.U., VI, 28. Gibault to Briand, June 20, 1772. A portion of this letter appears in translation in RACH, XX (1909), 420-21.

31 Father Hilaire de Genoveaux had been stationed at New Orleans, on and off, since 1752. He had been twice exiled from there because he was such a storm center. Returning to New Orleans from France in 1772, he was appointed pastor at Ste. Genevieve in 1773. True to his previous stormy career, he squabbled with his parishioners constantly until he took himself off in 1778. See Francis J. Yealy, *Sainte Genevieve: The Story of Missouri's Oldest Settlement* (Ste. Genevieve, Mo.: Bicentennial Historical Commission, 1935), pp. 52-57.

32 Pare and Quaife, "St. Joseph Baptismal Register," 236, 237, 239.

33 "Register of Marriages in the Parish of Michilimackinac, 1725-1821," *Wisconsin Historical Collections* XVIII (1908), 488.

34 Vincennes, Indiana, Old Cathedral Archives: Parish of St. Francis Xavier, parish records, 1770-1831.

35 *Wisconsin Historical Collections* XVIII (1908), 75-77.

36 RACH, XX (1909), 423. Gibault to Briand, December 4, 1775, from Detroit.

37  Ibid., 422. Gibault to Briand, October 9, 1775, from Michilimackinac.
38  Walter Havighurst, *Three Flags at the Straits* (Englewood Cliffs, N. J.: Prentice-Hall, 1966), pp. 94-96. Askin was something of a romantic character. He came to America from Ireland as a youth of nineteen. After serving with the British during the French and Indian War, he became a trader and settled at Michilimackinac in 1764. Soon he was a wealthy wholesaler with sloops of his own. He took an Ottawa woman into his home and fathered a rather numerous family. In 1772, while on a business trip to Detroit, he married Archange Berthe, the sister of his business partner, Jean-Baptiste Berthe. The record of the child's baptism, on October 3, 1775, may be found in *Wisconsin Historical Collections* XIX (1909), 77.
39  Têtu and Gagnon, *Mandements . . . des évêques de Québec,* II, 264-65. The document, issued on May 22, 1775, reads in part: "A group of subjects revolting against their legitimate sovereign . . . have come here to make trouble. . . . The singular goodness . . . with which we have been governed . . . is sufficient . . . to stimulate . . . your zeal to support . . . the crown. . . . Your oaths, your religion impose on you an indispensable obligation of defending your king. . . . Close your ears . . . do not heed the seditious who seek to draw you to evil. . . . The voice of your religion as well as your own interests are joined here. . . ."
40  Gibault was not forty years old, but thirty-eight.
41  RACH, XX (1909), 422, gives a translation of only two paragraphs of this lengthy letter, most of which is offered here in translation. The original may be consulted in AAQ, E.U., VI, 38.
42  AAQ, E.U., VI, 40. A translation of a portion of this letter appeared in RACH, XX (1909), 423-24.
43  Gosselin, *L'Eglise du Canada,* I, 335.
44  AAQ, E.U., VI, 42. Meurin to Briand, May 23, 1776, from Prairie du Rocher.
45  Gosselin, *L'Eglise du Canada,* I, 338. Briand to Gibault, April 26, 1777. The visitor was Jean-François Hubert who later became the bishop of Quebec. Though a native Canadian, Hubert had, up to that date, spent most of his sacerdotal career as a teacher in the diocesan seminary at Quebec.
46  IHC, XVI, 627. Gibault to Briand, August 26, 1777.

CHAPTER VI

1  John Law, *The Colonial History of Vincennes* (Vincennes, Ind.: Harvey Mason, 1858), p. 55.
2  Clarence W. Alvord, editor, *Kaskaskia Records, 1778-1790, Illinois State Historical Society Collections* V, *Virginia Series* II (Springfield: Illinois State Historical Library, 1909), xxxii. This source is henceforth cited as IHC, V.
3  James A. James, editor, *George Rogers Clark Papers, 1771-1781* (Springfield: Illinois State Historical Library, 1912), I, 31.
4  Edward G. Mason, editor, "Philippe François de Rastel, Chevalier de Rocheblave," *Chicago Historical Society's Collection* IV (1890), 383.
5  Ibid., 386.

6  Ibid., 385-88.
7  James, *Clark Papers*, I, 31.
8  Ibid., 34, 36.
9  Mason, "Rocheblave," 402, 410.
10 Ibid., 418-19.
11 Ibid., 416-17.
12 James, *Clark Papers*, I, 227-28.
13 Ibid., 230.
14 Ibid.
15 Ibid., 231.
16 Ibid., 233.
17 Ibid.
18 Ibid., 238.
19 Ibid.
20 Those who accompanied Gibault and Laffont were Captain Leonard Henry, Moses Henry, and Simon Kenton who was Clark's spy. See Fintan G. Walker, *The Catholic Church in the Meeting of Two Frontiers: The Southern Illinois Country (1763-1793)* (Washington, D. C.: Catholic University Press, 1935), p. 88.
21 Father Gibault baptized one of Laffont's children on July 9, 1778.
22 Walker, *Two Frontiers*, p. 89.
23 James, *Clark Papers*, I, 52.
24 Ibid., 54.
25 Ibid., 238.
26 Ibid., 56-59.
27 Ibid., 239.
28 Janet P. Shaw, "Francis Busseron," *Indiana Magazine of History* XXV (1929), 205.
29 James, *Clark Papers*, I, 177-78.
30 Ibid., 89. Leonard to Clark, December 17, 1778.
31 Ibid., 183.
32 Ibid., 90.
33 Ibid., 184. The "brother" was really Gibault's brother-in-law, Timothé Boucher de Montbrun.
34 IHC, V, xxvi. The document is dated August 8, 1778.
35 James, *Clark Papers*, I, 134.
36 Ibid., 136.
37 Ibid., 98. Clark to Patrick Henry, February 3, 1779.
38 Ibid., 139.
39 Têtu and Gagnon, *Mandements . . . des évêques de Québec*, II, 264-65.
40 A. M. Pope, "Father Floquet, the Canadian Friend of the American Patriots," RACH, V (1888), 63-65.
41 James, *Clark Papers*, I, 121.
42 Ibid.
43 Ibid., 230.
44 Ibid.
45 Ibid.

46   Ibid., 122. In his *Memoir,* written probably in 1790, Clark claimed for himself the honor of instigating the plan. See ibid., 237.

47   Clarence W. Alvord, "Father Gibault and the Submission of Post Vincennes, 1778," *American Historical Review* XIV (1908-1909), 550.

48   See Laffont's letter quoted in full below.

49   AAQ, E.U., VI, 45; IHC, V, 50-51.

50   AAQ, E.U., VI, 48; IHC, V, 520-21.

51   AAQ, E.U., VI, 68; IHC, V, 585.

52   AAQ, E.U., VI, 52; IHC, V, 541-42.

53   AAQ, E.U., VI, 68; IHC, V, 585.

54   See above, note 46.

55   James, *Clark Papers,* I, 241.

56   Ibid., II, 264. The amount mentioned included Laffont's expenses.

57   Ibid., 256.

58   George Herbermann and Henry F. Herbermann, "Very Reverend Pierre Gibault, V.G.," *Historical Records and Studies* VI (1912), pt. 2, 151.

59   Vincennes, Indiana, Old Cathedral Archives: Parish of St. Francis Xavier, parish records, 1770-1831.

60   James, *Clark Papers,* I, 87.

61   Ibid., 80.


CHAPTER VII

1   James, *Clark Papers,* I, 235.

2   The complete text of the act creating the county of Illinois may be studied in Clarence W. Alvord, editor, *Cahokia Records, 1778-1790, Illinois State Historical Society Collections* II, *Virginia Series* I (Springfield: Illinois State Historical Library, 1907), 9-10. This source is henceforth cited as IHC, II.

3   Ibid.

4   Ibid.

5   Ibid.

6   Though only twenty-eight when commissioned on December 12, 1778, John Todd's background amply prepared him to hold the office of county lieutenant. He was probably one of the few well-educated Americans on the frontier, having received a good classical education in a school conducted by his uncle, also John Todd. After his earlier education, Todd studied law and practiced for a short time. Attracted to the West, Todd was aide to General Lewis during Lord Dunmore's War. Settling in Kentucky, Todd was elected burgess from the county of Kentucky to the general assembly of Virginia during 1777. These duties prevented him from accompanying Clark to the Illinois Country, though his brother Levi was one of Clark's followers. See ibid., liii-iv.

7   Ibid., V, 82.

8   Ibid., 84.

9   Ibid.

10   Alvord, *Illinois Country,* pp. 336-37.

11  See IHC, II, lxxi, for a schedule of depreciations.

12  Todd recalled all paper money on July 27, 1779.

13  IHC, V, 131-32. The Continental Congress had recalled its own issues of May 20, 1777, and April 11, 1778. If not surrendered by the holders, the money was declared worthless.

14  Ibid., 89.

15  Ibid., 209.

16  Ibid., II, lxxix.

17  Legally, the county of Illinois ceased to exist in 1782.

18  Alvord, *Illinois Country*, p. 361.

19  IHC, II, cxx.

20  Carl E. Boyd, "The County of Illinois," *American Historical Review* IV (1898-1899), 633.

21  Jean-François Hubert was born at Quebec on February 23, 1739. The first candidate to the priesthood ordained by Bishop Briand, Hubert acted as the bishop's secretary for several years. He became rector of the Quebec seminary, an office he held in 1778. In 1781 he left the seminary and went to Detroit where he was missionary to the Indians until his appointment as coadjutor-bishop of Quebec in 1784. He returned to Quebec in 1785. He succeeded to the see on June 4, 1788, the day on which his predecessor, D'Esglis, died.

22  James, *Clark Papers*, I, 176.

23  This visit to Detroit may have been the reason why Hubert, wishing to be a missionary to the Indians, returned there in 1781.

24  AAQ, Ev.Q., I, 182. This is the Latin document. There exists, also, a French version, AAQ, E.U., VI, 46. The French text is much shorter and less detailed. Each text refers to the penalty imposed as suspension, not interdict. On the Latin text is written: "Sent to Detroit."

25  Gosselin, *L'Eglise du Canada*, I, 338.

26  Ibid., 339.

27  T. Lincoln Bouscaren and Adam C. Ellis, *Canon Law: A Text and Commentary* (Milwaukee: Bruce, 1957), pp. 879, 882.

28  IHC, II, 581. The land in question was given by Gibault to Stephen Trigg, one of Clark's officers, on April 21, 1779. On May 6 of that year Trigg transferred title to Clark. See ibid., V, 77-78, for the document of concession signed by Gibault. Clark, in turn, sold the land to Dorsey Pentecoste whose possession of it the Cahokians protested to Congress.

29  AAQ, E.U., VI, 55.

30  Joseph J. Thompson, "Illinois' First Citizen, Pierre Gibault," *Illinois Catholic Historical Review* VIII (1925-1926), 23.

31  Ibid., 24.

32  See AAQ, E.U., VI, 55.

33  Pierre Floquet was born at Paris on September 12, 1716, and entered the Society of Jesus on August 6, 1735. He reached Canada on August 17, 1744. He spent most of his active life as a missionary to the Indians settled around Montreal.

34 Laval Laurent, *Québec et l'Eglise aux Etats-Unis sous Mgr. Briand et Mgr. Plessis* (Washington, D. C.: Catholic University Press, 1945), p. 49. These two companies came to be called "Congress' Own." After the war some of the soldiers with their families, about 150 people in all, were given land near Cooperstown, New York. See John G. Shea, *The Life and Times of the Most Rev. John Carroll, Bishop and First Archbishop of Baltimore* (New York: The author, 1888), p. 268.

35 Ibid., p. 50.

36 Floquet was originally under suspicion because he publicly disapproved of the Quebec Act. He cooperated with the Americans, he attested, partly through simple fear and partly because he thought that if he aided the Americans they would not persecute his fellow Jesuits residing in Maryland and Pennsylvania. See Pope, "Father Floquet," 65-67.

37 James, *Clark Papers*, I, 175.

38 Ibid., 176.

39 *Michigan Pioneer and Historical Collections* IX (1886), 480. Hamilton to Haldimand, September 22, 1778.

40 James, *Clark Papers*, I, 292.

41 Louise P. Kellogg, *The British Régime in Wisconsin and the Northwest* (Madison: State Historical Society of Wisconsin, 1935), p. 163.

42 *Michigan Pioneer and Historical Collections* IX (1886), 527.

43 Ibid., 539. Sinclair to Brehm, February 15, 1780.

44 Ibid., 537. Brehm to Sinclair, April 17, 1780.

45 IHC, II, 585.

46 Ibid., V, 77-78.

47 Ibid., 519.

48 John Rothensteiner, *History of the Archdiocese of St. Louis in Its Various Stages from A.D. 1673 to A.D. 1928* (St. Louis: The author [?], 1928), I, 142.

49 IHC, V, 515. Jones to Hamtramck, October 29, 1789. John Rice Jones, a Welshman, educated at Oxford, came to Philadelphia in 1784 and went West in 1786, acting as commissary in Clark's expedition of that year. Jones refers to Father Thomas Le Dru, a Dominican who came to Canada from France in 1788. Later he migrated to the United States where Bishop Carroll granted him faculties, sending him to the Illinois Country. There Le Dru incited all sorts of ecclesiastical trouble and soon departed. See Laurent, *Mgr. Briand et Mgr. Plessis*, p. 101.

50 IHC, II, 121. Lafleur was a resident of Kaskaskia. See ibid., V, 417, note 36.

51 Rothensteiner, *Archdiocese of St. Louis*, I, 112.

52 Ibid.

53 Ste. Genevieve parish records.

54 Louis Houck, *The Spanish Régime in Missouri* (Chicago: Donnelley, 1909), I, 61.

55 Ibid., 70-71. The judgment is very unfair since Piernas hardly had time to have become really acquainted with the people. Also, he was newly come from Spain and had no experience with the difficulties of frontier living.

56 NMA, XI, 1431. The original of the will appears to have been lost. The Society possesses a copy of the document.

57 McDermott, in his article, "Library of Father Gibault," pp. 273-75, gives a complete list of the contents of the library.

58 NMA, XI, 1431.

59 Ibid.

60 IHC, V, 540-41. Historians have been unable to determine accurately which governor Gibault had in mind.

61 James, *Clark Papers*, II, 211-12.

62 IHC, V, 520-21; AAQ, E.U., VI, 48.

CHAPTER VIII

1 Peter Guilday, *The Life and Times of John Carroll, Archbishop of Baltimore (1735-1815)* (Westminster, Md.: Newman, 1954), p. 146. Exercise of ecclesiastical jurisdiction over the colonies by the vicar apostolic of London seems to have developed from simple custom. In 1756, the proper papal office, the Sacred Congregation of Propaganda, asked Bishop Petre by what authority he exercised such jurisdiction. He replied that he did so on the logical assumption that the colonies were his responsibility. Thereupon Rome granted the vicar apostolic of London jurisdiction and renewed the grant on March 25, 1757.

2 Ibid., p. 164. Talbot stated his position in 1783 when two American priests, John Boone and Henry Pile, applied for spiritual faculties before leaving London on their way home. Talbot exercised no authority over the Catholics in America from the very beginning of the Revolution. He may have been influenced in this by his brother, the earl of Shrewsbury. Perhaps, like Briand in Canada, Talbot wished to avoid any accusation that Catholics were not loyal to the crown. However, Talbot did not lack courage for he was twice brought to trial during his episcopate, charged with the crime of saying Mass in his house. On each occasion he was acquitted for lack of evidence. He was the last priest so tried in England. During the Gordon Riots in 1780, Lord Mansfield, the judge who acquitted Talbot, had his house sacked, though the judge was no friend of the Catholics.

3 Shea, *John Carroll*, p. 209. Shea quotes the document which had no date. The presumption is, of course, that the petition was sent in late November or December 1783.

4 Ibid., p. 224.

5 Ibid., p. 225. Leonardo Cardinal Antonelli, Prefect of Propaganda to Talbot, June 19, 1784.

6 Ste. Genevieve parish records. The last entry made by Father Gibault was on November 2, 1784. On that day he baptized a Negro infant.

7 John Rothensteiner, "Paul de Saint Pierre, the First German-American Priest of the West," *Catholic Historical Review* V (1919-1920), 197. It is not at all surprising that de Saint Pierre entered a French convent since the southern border of the duchy of Zweibrucken was not five miles from the

border of France. Father de Saint Pierre was born in 1751, according to Gibault, who said the Carmelite was thirty-seven in 1786. See IHC, V, 547.

8  Rothensteiner, "Paul de Saint Pierre," 197. One of the four regiments landing in Rhode Island with Rochambeau was the Régiment de Royal Deux-Ponts. The French title is an exact translation of the German Zweibrucken.

9  Rothensteiner, *Archdiocese of St. Louis*, I, 156-57. Ferdinand Farmer, at Philadelphia, to John Carroll, at Baltimore, October 9, 1784. Father Farmer, Carroll's vicar-general, was himself a German. His name was really Steinmeyer. Born in Germany on October 13, 1720, he became a Jesuit in 1743 and was sent to Maryland in 1758. He died at Philadelphia on August 17, 1786.

10  Rothensteiner, "Paul de Saint Pierre," 201.

11  Father de Saint Pierre remained in the Mississippi Valley until 1797. He then moved to Louisiana where he died at Iberville in 1826.

12  *Relations*, LXX, 235, 237, gives the number of houses in 1762. See Beverley W. Bond, "Two Westward Journeys of John Filson," *Mississippi Valley Historical Review* IX (1922-1923), 326. In his journal, written in 1785, Filson says that there were upwards of 300 houses at Vincennes.

13  Bond, "John Filson," 330.

14  AAQ, E.U., VI, 53; IHC, V, 534-35.

15  AAQ, E.U., VI, 53; IHC, V, 535-36.

16  AAQ, E.U., VI, 53; IHC, V, 542-43.

17  AAQ, E.U., VI, 53; IHC, V, 544.

18  AAQ, E.U., VI, 53; IHC, V, 536-37.

19  AAQ, E.U., VI, 53; IHC, V, 546.

20  AAQ, E.U., VI, 53; IHC, V, 546-47.

21  AAQ, E.U., VI, 53; IHC, V, 547.

22  AAQ, E.U., VI, 53. The rest of Gibault's letter of June 6, 1768, is given in IHC, V, 534-47. The first paragraph, presented here, has not previously been available.

23  AAQ, E.U., VI, 53; IHC, V, 557-58.

24  AAQ, E.U., VI, 53; IHC, V, 539-40.

25  AAQ, E.U., VI, 53; IHC, V, 541-42.

26  AAQ, E.U., VI, 53; IHC, V, 544-45.

27  Vincennes, Indiana, Old Cathedral Archives: Parish of St. Francis Xavier, parish records, 1770-1831.

28  Ibid.

29  J. B. Culemans, "Father de la Valinière, 'Rebel' and Illinois Missionary," *Illinois Catholic Historical Review* I (1918-1919), 339-51.

30  IHC, V, 548. De la Valinière to the Inhabitants of Cahokia, October 17, 1786.

31  Ibid., 549-54. De la Valinière to Joseph Labuxière, April 11, 1787.

32  Ibid., 580.

33  Ibid., 568-69.

34  Ibid., 558.

35  Ibid., 559.

36  Shea, *John Carroll*, pp. 431-32.

37   AAQ, E.U., I, 1; IHC, V, 581-82.
38   In his letter of June 6, 1786, Gibault had asked the bishop for a decision on several cases of conscience. This is the meaning of the reference here.
39   AAQ, E.U., VI, 68; IHC, V, 583-86.
40   IHC, V, 589-90.
41   Practically nothing is known about Le Dru except that he came to Canada from France and was employed there briefly. Then he went to Baltimore where Carroll sent him to the West in 1789. Le Dru removed to St. Louis in November 1789, remaining there until 1795. Apparently he then went to Detroit. Writing to Carroll, on May 2, 1796, Bishop Hubert remarked: ". . . an apostate Dominican named Le Dru, [has] succeeded in imbuing some of the officers of the American troops posted near Detroit with prejudice against [the] priest . . ." See Shea, *John Carroll*, p. 479. The priest to whom Hubert referred was Father Edmund Burke, then missionary to the Indians around Detroit and later a bishop in Nova Scotia.
42   Thomas T. McAvoy, *The Catholic Church in Indiana, 1789-1834* (New York: Columbia University Press, 1940), pp. 57-58.
43   IHC, II, 589-90. Joseph Labuxière came to the Illinois Country from Canada. In 1757 he was appointed notary clerk and served the French government until 1765. He migrated to St. Louis then and remained in Spanish territory until 1781 when he returned to Kaskaskia and was appointed state's attorney. He died on April 29, 1791. See ibid., 625.
44   Ibid., 624-32. Census of 1787. The population of Cahokia at that time was 239 males. Alvord, in his *Illinois Country*, p. 407, reports that in 1790 the total population of Cahokia was 467.
45   See IHC, II, 607-08. Ordinance of July 5, 1789.
46   AAQ, E.U., I, 2; IHC, V, 590-91. The two letters sent by Gibault have not been found nor has the one which Carroll says he sent to Gibault.
47   AAQ, E.U., I, 2; IHC, V, 592.
48   AAQ, E.U., I, 2; IHC, V, 592. Father de Saint Pierre exercised ecclesiastical jurisdiction quite validly. The decree appointing Carroll superior of all priests in the United States also granted all then present faculties to exercise the sacred ministries. De Saint Pierre had been in America for some years before the decree was issued on June 9, 1784. However, since the Roman document seemed to allow Carroll to delegate faculties to those priests only who were sent to America by the Sacred Congregation of Propaganda, there was a question in Carroll's mind whether he could grant de Saint Pierre faculties since the latter had been sent on French authority. The matter was later clarified when it was discovered that by a bureaucratic error a formula applying only to Africa had been used for the United States. See Shea, *John Carroll*, p. 246.
49   Alvord, *Illinois Country*, p. 417.
50   William H. Smith, *The St. Clair Papers: The Life and Public Service of Arthur St. Clair* (Cincinnati: Clarke, 1882), I, 148-49.
51   See Alvord, *Illinois Country*, p. 418. Congress solved the problem by granting, out of hand, 400 acres to each head of a family residing in the Illinois Country in 1783.

52 Smith, *St. Clair Papers*, II, 179.
53 Gibault's lengthy memorial is given, complete, by Thompson, "Pierre Gibault," 4-5.
54 IHC, V, 597. Carroll to Gibault, January 23, 1792.
55 Ibid., 599. Carroll to Hubert, January 23, 1792. Carroll mistakenly called Cahokia Vincennes here. The bill clearly gives Gibault ". . . two lots of land heretofore in the occupation of the priests at Cahokia . . ." See *United States Statutes at Large* I, 221-22. Though he was granted the small piece of land on March 3, 1791, Gibault probably never took advantage of his property. It is quite likely that he did not learn of the success of his petition until he had left Cahokia to take up residence at New Madrid.
56 IHC, V, 598.
57 Ibid., 515. Jones to Hamtramck, October 29, 1789. The site on which New Madrid was built is thought to have been called L'Anse a la Graise, or Grease Cove because of the character of the soil there.

CHAPTER IX

1 Alcée Fortier, *A History of Louisiana* (Paris: Goupil, 1904), I, 149-50. Louis XV to Dabbadie, April 21, 1764.
2 Roger Baudier, *The Catholic Church in Louisiana* (New Orleans: The author, 1939), p. 174. La Balize was a small village situated very close to the mouth of the Mississippi River. The place was about a hundred miles as the crow flies from New Orleans.
3 O'Reilly, probably born at Dublin in 1722, was a soldier of fortune who served successively in the armies of Spain, Austria, and France. In 1761 he rejoined the Spanish army. After returning to Spain from Louisiana in 1770, he commanded an unsuccessful Spanish expedition against the Algerians, 1774-1775. In 1786 he was deprived of military command and accused of plotting against the Spanish crown. He died near Chinchilla in Spain on March 23, 1794.
4 Charles Gayarré, *History of Louisiana* (New York: Widdleton, 1867), III, 15-18.
5 Fortier, *Louisiana*, II, 8. The diocese of Santiago de Cuba was established in 1518 with responsibility for Cuba and Florida.
6 Baudier, *Catholic Church in Louisiana*, p. 184.
7 Father Dagobert was fully justified in refusing to recognize Cyrillo's authority since it arose from the purely civil government of Spain. Spanish Louisiana was not placed under the authority of the bishop of Santiago de Cuba by Rome until 1777. See Rothensteiner, *Archdiocese of St. Louis*, I, 111.
8 Baudier, *Catholic Church in Louisiana*, p. 200.
9 Fortier, *Louisiana*, II, 115.
10 Max Savelle, *George Morgan, Colony Builder* (New York: AMS Press, 1967), p. 202.
11 Ibid., p. 201.
12 Ibid., p. 5.

13  Ibid., p. 201. Morgan offered one third of a dollar per acre, but Congress demanded two thirds of a dollar.
14  Houck, *Spanish Régime*, II, 110.
15  Savelle, *George Morgan*, p. 206.
16  Houck, *Spanish Régime*, I, 309.
17  Ibid., 328-29.
18  Ibid., II, 393-97.
19  Gayarré, *Louisiana*, III, 406.
20  Rothensteiner, "Paul de Saint Pierre," 195.
21  Father Gibault's last entry in the parish registers at Cahokia was made on October 17, 1791. On that day he presided at a burial.
22  Shea, *John Carroll*, p. 481.
23  NMA, XI, 1431.
24  Ibid., 1431-34.
25  F. G. Holwick, "The Arkansas Mission under Rosati," *St. Louis Catholic Historical Review* I (1918-1919), 243.
26  NMA, XI, 1431-36. Father Patrick Walsh was one of several priests of Irish extraction sent to Louisiana in 1792 by the king of Spain in the hope that these men who spoke English as well as Spanish might convert the Americans entering the Spanish colony.
27  Baudier, *Catholic Church in Louisiana*, p. 224.
28  St. Louis Archdiocesan Archives: Henry Van der Sanden, "Sacerdotes Saeculares, 1670-1900," p. 28.
29  NMA, XI, 1431-36.
30  Ibid.
31  Rothensteiner, *Archdiocese of St. Louis*, I, 177.
32  Houck, *Spanish Régime*, I, 336.
33  John Rothensteiner, "Historical Sketch of Catholic New Madrid," *St. Louis Catholic Historical Review* IV (1922), 120.
34  Baudier, *Catholic Church in Louisiana*, p. 225.
35  The story of the colony is well related in an article by Laurence J. Kenny, "The Gallipolis Colony (1790)," *Catholic Historical Review* IV (1918-1919), 415-51.
36  NMA, XI, 1431-56.
37  Ibid., 1431-37. Walsh to Gibault, May 15, 1794.
38  Arthur P. Whitaker, *The Spanish-American Frontier: 1783-1795* (Boston: Houghton-Mifflin, 1927), pp. 211-13.
39  NMA, XI, 1431-44.
40  Ibid.
41  John Rothensteiner, "Father James Maxwell of Ste. Genevieve," *St. Louis Catholic Historical Review* IV (1922), 142-54.
42  NMA, XI, 1431-46.
43  Ibid., 1431-53.
44  The sacrament of matrimony is not conferred by the priest, but by the two contracting parties. The priest is merely the official witness for the Church.
45  NMA, XI, 1431-67.
46  Rothensteiner, *Archdiocese of St. Louis*, I, 182.

47 Van der Sanden, "Sacerdotes Saeculares," p. 28.

48 NMA, XI, 1416. Peñalver to Gibault, May 6, 1797.

49 St. Isidore was a twelfth-century Spanish peasant farmer. He died near Madrid on May 15, 1130.

50 Houck, *Spanish Régime*, II, 338.

51 Ibid., 339-40. See also pp. 351-52, wherein is listed the contents of the church at New Madrid.

52 NMA, XI, 1418.

53 Ibid., 1431-77.

54 Ibid., 1431-67.

55 Ibid., 1426.

56 Ibid., V, 1115-25. See also McDermott, "Library of Father Gibault," 273.

57 NMA, V, 1115-25. Gibault's effects were auctioned on April 3, 1803. His library was purchased by Joseph Michel, a New Madrid merchant.


### DOCUMENT I

1 The inventory of Father Gibault's effects and the bill of sale of his books is found in NMA 1115, VI, 259 ff.

2 This work does not seem to be identifiable.

3 The works to which the entry referred appear to be:

Mathieu Beuvelet, *Meditations sur les principales veritez chrestiennes et ecclésiastiques pour tous les dimanches, festes et autres jours.* The work was first published at Paris in 1651.

Julien de Hayneuf, *Meditations pour les temps.* It was first published in 1661.

Alphonsus Rodriquez, *The Practice of Christian Perfection.* This three-volume work, originally appearing in Spanish in 1606, went through innumerable editions in almost every European language.

4 Dom Augustin Calmet (1672-1707) was an illustrious French Benedictine. The work which Gibault had was probably Calmet's *Histoire de l'Ancien et du Nouveau Testament.*

5 Lamette seems to have been an obscure author whose work did not find its way into any great depository. Germain Fromageau's book was probably his *Le dictionnaire des cas de conscience* (Paris, 1733).

6 This was Jean Pontas who published *Dictionnaire de cas de conscience* (Paris, 1715).

7 Concerning de Hayneuf, see above, note 3.

8 No information regarding these three authors seems to be available.

9 Jean Baptiste Massillon (1663-1742) preached on several occasions before Louis XV. He was bishop of Clermont, 1719-1742. A collection of his sermons was published in 1745 by his nephew.

10 Louis Bourdaloue (1632-1704) was a noted preacher at Paris, 1699-1703. After his death his sermons were edited by Bretonneau at Paris, 1707-1721. The work was composed of fourteen volumes.

11 This work does not seem to be identifiable.

12 The thirty-five-volume work on ecclesiastical history was, undoubtedly, Claude Fleury's *Histoire ecclésiastique*. During his lifetime, 1640-1725, Fleury published twenty volumes covering the period from the Ascension of Christ to 1414. These were published between 1691 and 1720. After Fleury's death, Jean Claude Fabre continued the work, publishing sixteen volumes between 1722 and 1736. These brought the work down to 1595.

## DOCUMENT II

1 The original of this letter is preserved in the archives of Notre Dame University, Notre Dame, Indiana.

2 The bishop is quoting Matthew 10:16 which, in English, reads: "Behold, I send you as sheep in the midst of wolves. Be ye therefore wise as serpents and simple as doves."

3 In the original, this sentence appears in Latin: *Esto ovis, ut lupi, ad quos te mitto, missus ego a Xto Jesu, fiant oves.*

4 Briand is quoting James 1:18.

5 The phrase in quotations is taken from the first phrase of 2 Timothy 4:2.

6 This is the remainder of 2 Timothy 4:2.

7 The bishop seems to be referring to Isaias 60:12.

8 This frequently quoted sentence is from 1 Corinthians 3:7.

9 By "the general," the bishop undoubtedly meant the British governor-general of Canada.

10 Here, the bishop conjoined two biblical quotations. The first portion, "they who serve," is found in 1 Corinthians 9:13. The second part, "the laborer," is found in Luke 10:7.

11 The bishop is referring to canonical impediments to marriage which the Catholic Church dispenses under certain circumstances.

12 See above, note 11.

# BIBLIOGRAPHY

GUIDES TO ARCHIVAL MATERIAL

Alvord, Clarence W. "Eighteenth Century French Records in the Archives of Illinois." *Annual Report of the American Historical Association for the Year 1905.* Washington, D.C.: Government Printing Office, 1906. pp. 353-66.

Beers, Henry P. *The French and the British in the Old Northwest: A Bibliographical Guide to Archives and Manuscript Sources.* Detroit: Wayne University Press, 1964. 297 pp.

Doughty, Arthur G. "Sources for the History of the Catholic Church in the Public Archives of Canada." *Catholic Historical Review* XIX (1933-1934), 148-68.

Holwick, F. G. "The Historical Archives of the Archdiocese of St. Louis." *St. Louis Catholic Historical Review* I (1918-1919), 24-29.

Linsay, Lionel S. "The Archives of the Archdiocese of Quebec." *Records of the American Catholic Historical Society of Philadelphia* XVIII (1907), 8-11.

### ARCHIVAL MATERIALS

Baltimore, Archdiocesan Archives. Letter of Bishop Carroll to Father Gibault, June 5, 1792; Letter of Father Gabriel Richard to Bishop Carroll, May 11, 1804.

Cahokia, Illinois, Parish of the Holy Family. Register of burials, 1783-1819.

Missouri Historical Society of St. Louis. New Madrid Archives, V, XI.

Notre Dame University, Notre Dame, Indiana. Original of a letter of Bishop Briand to Father Gibault, May 15, 1768.

Prairie du Rocher, Illinois, Parish of St. Joseph. Registers of baptisms, marriages, and burials, 1765-1799.

Quebec, Archdiocesan Archives: Etats-Unis. This depository contains the largest single collection of manuscript material on Gibault.

St. Louis, Archdiocesan Archives. Manuscript copy of Father Henry Van der Sanden's "Sacerdotes Saeculares, 1670-1900."

St. Louis, Old Cathedral Parish. Register of baptisms, 1764-1781.

St. Louis University, St. Louis, Missouri. "Registre de la Paroisse de la Conception de Notre Dame Des Cascaskias," "Registre des Baptemes Dans L'Eglise de L'Immaculee Conception aux Cascaskias, April 27, 1759-June 18, 1815," "Registre des Mariages dans L'Eglise de Notre Dame de L'Immaculee Conception aux Kaskaskias, November 20, 1741-February 10, 1834." These three original volumes are the property of the Diocese of Belleville, but are on deposit at St. Louis University.

Ste. Genevieve, Missouri, Ste. Genevieve Parish. "Liber Baptismorum Parochiae Stae. Genovefae ab Anno 1760 ad Annum 1786," "Liber Baptismorum Parociae Stae. Genevefae ab Anno 1786 ad Annum 1820."

Vincennes, Indiana, Old Cathedral Archives. Parish of St. Francis Xavier, parish records, 1770-1831.

PUBLISHED PRIMARY SOURCES

Alvord, Clarence W., editor. *Cahokia Records, 1778-1790. Illinois State Historical Society Collections* II, *Virginia Series* I. Springfield: Illinois State Historical Library, 1907. 663 pp.

———— *Kaskaskia Records, 1778-1790. Illinois State Historical Society Collections* V, *Virginia Series* II. Springfield: Illinois State Historical Library, 1909. 681 pp.

Alvord, Clarence W., and Clarence E. Carter, editors. *The Critical Period, 1763-1765. Illinois State Historical Society Collections* X, *British Series* I. Springfield: Illinois State Historical Library, 1915. 591 pp.

———— *The New Régime, 1765-1767. Illinois State Historical Society Collections* XI, *British Series* II. Springfield: Illinois State Historical Library, 1916. 700 pp.

———— *Trade and Politics, 1767-1769. Illinois State Historical Society Collections* XVI, *British Series* III. Springfield: Illinois State Historical Library, 1921. 760 pp.

Bond, Beverley W. "Two Westward Journeys of John Filson." *Mississippi Valley Historical Review* IX (1922-1923), 320-30.

"Correspondence between the Sees of Quebec and Baltimore, 1788-1847." *Records of the American Catholic Historical Society of Philadelphia* XVIII (1907), 155-89, 282-305, 343-67.

Flagg, Edmund. "The Far West: Or a Tour Beyond the Mountains." In Reuben G. Thwaites, editor, *Early Western Travels*. Cleveland: Clark, 1906. XXVI, XXVII. 2 vols.

Houck, Louis. *The Spanish Régime in Missouri*. Chicago: Donnelley, 1909. 2 vols.

Hughes, Thomas A. *The History of the Society of Jesus in North America*. New York: Longmans, 1908-1917. 4 vols.

"Inventaire de la correspondance de Mgr. Jean-Olivier Briand, évêque de Québec." *Rapport de l'archiviste de la Province de Québec*, 1929-1930. pp. 47-136.

James, James A., editor. *George Rogers Clark Papers, 1771-1781*. Springfield: Illinois State Historical Library, 1912. 2 vols.

Kellogg, Louise P. *Early Narratives of the Northwest, 1634-1699*. New York: Scribner's, 1917. 382 pp.

"Letters from Lieutenant-Governor Hamilton to General Haldimand." *Michigan Pioneer and Historical Collections* IX (1886), 430-87.

"Letters from the Archdiocesan Archives at Quebec." *Records of the American Catholic Historical Society of Philadelphia* XX (1909), 326-430.

McDermott, John Francis. "The Library of Father Gibault." *Mid-America* XVII (1935), 273-75.

————, editor. *Old Cahokia: A Narrative and Documents Illustrating the First Century of Its History*. St. Louis: Historical Documents Foundation, 1949. 355 pp.

Mason, Edward G. "John Todd Papers." *Chicago Historical Society's Collection* IV (1890), 285-359.

Nasatir, Abraham P., and Ernest R. Liljegren. "Materials Relating to the History of the Mississippi Valley from the Minutes of the Spanish Supreme Council of State, 1787-1797." *Louisiana Historical Quarterly* XXI (1938), 5-75.

Pare, George, and Milo M. Quaife, editors. "The St. Joseph Baptismal Register." *Mississippi Valley Historical Review* XIII (1926-1927), 201-39.

Quaife, Milo M., editor. *The Capture of Old Vincennes, the Original Narratives of George Rogers Clark and His Opponent General Henry Hamilton.* Indianapolis: Bobbs-Merrill, 1927. 231 pp.

"Register of Marriages in the Parish of Michilimackinac, 1725-1821." *Wisconsin Historical Collections* XVIII (1908), 469-513.

"Register of the Baptisms of the Mission of St. Ignace de Michilimackinac, 1695-1821." *Wisconsin Historical Collections* XIX (1909), 1-148.

Saint-Vallier, Jean-Baptiste de la Croix Chevriers. *Estat présent de l'eglise et de la colonie française dans la Nouvelle-France.* Paris: Coté, 1856. 102 pp.

Smith, William H. *The St. Clair Papers: The Life and Public Service of Arthur St. Clair.* Cincinnati: Clarke, 1882. 2 vols.

Stoddard, Amos. *Sketches, Historical and Descriptive of Louisiana.* Philadelphia: Carey, 1812. 488 pp.

Têtu, H., and C. O. Gagnon, editors. *Mandements, lettres pastorales et circulaires des évêques de Québec.* Quebec: The editors, 1887-1890. 6 vols.

Thwaites, Reuben G., editor. *The Jesuit Relations and Allied Documents.* Cleveland: Burrows, 1896-1901. 73 vols.

*United States Statutes at Large.* Vol. I.

SECONDARY SOURCES, BOOKS

Alvord, Clarence Walworth. *The Illinois Country 1673-1818.* Chicago: Loyola University Press, 1965. 524 pp.

Armour, David A., editor. *Treason at Michilimackinac.* Mackinac Island, Mich.: Mackinac Island State Park Commission, 1967. 103 pp.

Baudier, Roger. *The Catholic Church in Louisiana.* New Orleans: The author, 1939. 605 pp.

Belting, Natalia M. *Kaskaskia under the French Regime.* Urbana: University of Illinois Press, 1948. 140 pp.

Bouscaren, T. Lincoln, and Adam C. Ellis. *Canon Law: A Text and Commentary.* Milwaukee: Bruce, 1957. 980 pp.

Carpenter, Allen. *Illinois, Land of Lincoln.* Chicago: Children's Press, 1968. 207 pp.

Carter, Clarence E. *Great Britain and the Illinois Country, 1763-1774.* Washington, D. C.: American Historical Association, 1910. 223 pp.

Crétineau-Joly, Jacques. *Histoire religieuse, politique et littéraire de la Compagnie de Jésus.* Paris: Poussielgue-Rusand, 1854. 5 vols.

Delanglez, Jean. *The French Jesuits in Lower Louisiana (1700-1763).* Washington, D. C.: Catholic University Press, 1935. 574 pp.

Derlath, August W. *Vincennes, Portal to the West.* Englewood Cliffs, N. J.: Prentice-Hall, 1968. 201 pp.

Dispense, James. *Forgotten Patriot.* Notre Dame, Ind.: DuJarie, 1966. 95 pp.

Donnelly, Joseph P. *Jacques Marquette, S.J., 1637-1675.* Chicago: Loyola University Press, 1968. 395 pp.

———— *The Parish of the Holy Family, Cahokia, Illinois, 1699-1949.* Cahokia, Ill.: 250th Anniversary Association, 1949. 62 pp.

————, editor. "Burial Records of the Holy Family Church." In John Francis McDermott, editor, *Old Cahokia.* St. Louis: Historical Documents Foundation, 1949. pp. 255-85.

———— "The Founding of the Holy Family Mission and Its History in the Eighteenth Century: Documents." In John Francis McDermott, editor, *Old Cahokia.* St. Louis: Historical Documents Foundation, 1949. pp. 55-92.

———— "Letters from Monk's Mound: The Correspondence of Dom Urban Guillet with Bishop Plessis of Quebec, 1809-1812." In John Francis McDermott, editor, *Old Cahokia*. St. Louis: Historical Documents Foundation, 1949. pp. 286-320.

Douville, Raymond, and Jacques-Donat Casanova. *Daily Life in Early Canada*. New York: Macmillan, 1968. 224 pp.

Fakhry, Ahmed. *The Pyramids*. Chicago: University of Chicago Press, 1961. 260 pp.

Fortier, Alcée. *A History of Louisiana*. Paris: Goupil, 1904. 4 vols.

Franzwa, Gregory M. *The Story of Old Ste. Genevieve*. St. Louis: Patrice Press, 1967. 169 pp.

Garraghan, Gilbert J. *Chapters in Frontier History*. Milwaukee: Bruce, 1934. 188 pp.

———— *The Jesuits of the Middle United States*. New York: America Press, 1938. 3 vols.

Gayarré, Charles. *History of Louisiana*. New York: Widdleton, 1867. 4 vols.

Glasson, Ernest. *Précis elémentaire de l'histoire du droit français*. Paris: Chaumont, 1874. 473 pp.

Gosselin, Amédée. *L'Instruction au Canada sous le régime français (1635-1760)*. Quebec: Laflamme, 1911. 501 pp.

Gosselin, Auguste. *L'Eglise du Canada après la conquête*. Quebec: Laflamme, 1916-1917. 2 vols.

Guilday, Peter. *The Life and Times of John Carroll, Archbishop of Baltimore (1735-1815)*. Westminster, Md.: Newman, 1954. 864 pp.

Harney, Martin P. *The Jesuits in History*. New York: America Press, 1941. 513 pp.

Havighurst, Walter. *Three Flags at the Straits*. Englewood Cliffs, N. J.: Prentice-Hall, 1966. 219 pp.

Heinrich, Pierre. *La Louisiane sous la Compagnie des Indes, 1717-1731*. Paris: Librairie Orientale and Americaine, 1908. 298 pp.

Houck, Louis. *A History of Missouri*. Chicago: Donnelley, 1908. 3 vols.

Kellogg, Louise P. *The British Régime in Wisconsin and the Northwest*. Madison: State Historical Society of Wisconsin, 1935. 361 pp.

Lanctôt, Gustave. *A History of Canada*. Cambridge: Harvard University Press, 1963-1965. 3 vols.

Lareau, Edmund. *Histoire du droit canadien depuis les origines de la colonie jusqu'à nos jours*. Montreal: The author [?], 1888. 2 vols.

Launay, Adrien. *Histoire générale de la Société des Missions-Etrangères*. Paris: The author [?], 1894. 3 vols.

Laurent, Laval. *Québec et l'Eglise aux Etats-Unis sous Mgr. Briand et Mgr. Plessis*. Washington, D.C.: Catholic University Press, 1945. 258 pp.

Laurière, Emile. *Histoire de la Louisiane française, 1673-1939*. Paris: Maisonneuve, 1940. 445 pp.

Law, John. *The Colonial History of Vincennes*. Vincennes, Ind.: Harvey Mason, 1858. 156 pp.

McAvoy, Thomas T. *The Catholic Church in Indiana, 1789-1834*. New York: Columbia University Press, 1940. 226 pp.

Metzger, Charles H. *Catholics and the American Revolution*. Chicago: Loyola University Press, 1962. 306 pp.

Quaife, Milo M., editor. *The Western Country in the 17th Century*. Chicago: Lakeside Press, 1947. 161 pp.

Rochemonteix, Camille de. *Les Jésuites de la Nouvelle-France au XVIIIe siècle*. Paris: Picard, 1906. 2 vols.

Roemer, Theodore. *The Catholic Church in the United States*. St. Louis: Herder, 1950. 444 pp.

Rothensteiner, John. *History of the Archdiocese of St. Louis in Its Various Stages from A.D. 1673 to A.D. 1928.* St. Louis: The author [?], 1928. 2 vols.

Savelle, Max. *George Morgan, Colony Builder.* New York: AMS Press, 1967. 266 pp.

Schlarman, J. H. *From Quebec to New Orleans.* Belleville, Ill.: Buechler, 1929. 569 pp.

Shea, John G. *The Catholic Church in Colonial Days.* New York: The author, 1886. 663 pp.

———— *The Life and Times of the Most Rev. John Carroll, Bishop and First Archbishop of Baltimore.* New York: The author, 1888. 695 pp.

Silverberg, Robert. *Mound Builders of Ancient America.* New York: Graphic Arts, 1968. 369 pp.

Surrey, N. M. *The Commerce of Louisiana during the French Régime, 1699-1763.* New York: Longmans, 1916. 476 pp.

Tanguay, Cyprien. *Dictionnaire généalogique des familles canadiennes depuis la fondation de la colonie jusqu'à nos jours.* Montreal: Senécal, 1871-1880. 7 vols.

Temple, Wayne C. *Indian Villages in the Illinois Country.* Springfield: Illinois State Museum, 1958. 218 pp.

Villiers de Terrage, Marc de. *Les dernières années de la Louisiane française.* Paris: Guilmoto, 1904. 408 pp.

Vogel, Claude L. *The Capuchins in French Louisiana (1723-1766).* Washington, D.C.: Catholic University Press, 1928. 201 pp.

Walker, Fintan G. *The Catholic Church in the Meeting of Two Frontiers: The Southern Illinois Country (1763-1793).* Washington, D.C.: Catholic University Press, 1935. 169 pp.

Whitaker, Arthur P. *The Spanish-American Frontier: 1783-1795.* Boston: Houghton-Mifflin, 1927. 255 pp.

Wilson, William E. *Indiana, a History.* Bloomington: Indiana University Press, 1966. 243 pp.

Yealy, Francis J. *Sainte Genevieve: The Story of Missouri's Oldest Settlement.* Ste. Genevieve, Mo.: Bicentennial Historical Commission, 1935. 145 pp.

SECONDARY SOURCES,
PERIODICAL LITERATURE

Alvord, Clarence W. "Father Gibault and the Submission of Post Vincennes, 1778." *American Historical Review* XIV (1908-1909), 544-57.

———— "The Oath of Vincennes, 1778." *Illinois Historical Society Transactions,* 1907, pp. 265-76.

Beuckman, Frederick. "The Commons of Kaskaskia, Cahokia and Prairie du Rocher." *Illinois Catholic Historical Review* I (1918-1919), 405-12.

———— "Ecclesiastical Jurisdiction in Illinois." *Illinois Catholic Historical Review* I (1918-1919), 64-71.

Boyd, Carl E. "The County of Illinois." *American Historical Review* IV (1898-1899), 623-35.

Brown, Stuart. "Old Kaskaskia Days and Ways." *Illinois Catholic Historical Review* I (1918-1919), 413-23; II (1919-1920), 61-73.

Callen, Louise. "Patriot Priest." *Missouri Historical Society Bulletin* V (1949), 266-88.

Campbell, Thomas. "The Beginnings of the Hierarchy in the United States." *Historical Records and Studies* I (1899), 251-77.

Culemans, J. B. "Father de la Valinière, 'Rebel' and Illinois Missionary." *Illinois Catholic Historical Review* I (1918-1919), 339-51.

Dunn, Jacob P. "Father Gibault: The Patriot Priest of the Northwest." *Illinois Historical Society Transactions,* 1905, pp. 15-34.

———— "The Mission to the Oubache." *Indiana State Historical Society Publications* III (1895), 256-330.

Fleureau, Louis. "La famille Margane de Lavaltrie." *Bulletin des Recherches Historiques* XXIII (1917), 33-53.

Garraghan, Gilbert J. "Old Vincennes, a Chapter in the Ecclesiastical History of the West." *Mid-America* II (1931), 3-19.

Hebermann, George, and Henry F. Hebermann. "Very Reverend Pierre Gibault, V.G." *Historical Records and Studies* VI (1912), 130-65.

Holwick, F. G. "The Arkansas Mission under Rosati." *St. Louis Catholic Historical Review* I (1918-1919), 243-67.

Hughes, Thomas. "The London Vicariate-Apostolic and the West Indies." *Dublin Review* CXXIV (1914), 67-93.

Hynes, Robert. "The Old Church at Cahokia." *Illinois Catholic Historical Review* I (1918-1919), 459-63.

Kenny, Laurence J. "The Gallipolis Colony (1790)." *Catholic Historical Review* IV (1918-1919), 415-51.

Lambeling, A. A. "Very Reverend Pierre Gibault, the Patriot Priest." *Records of the American Catholic Historical Society of Philadelphia* I (1885), 56-58.

Mason, Edward G., editor. "Philippe François de Rastel, Chevalier de Rocheblave." *Chicago Historical Society's Collection* IV (1890), 360-419.

Metzger, Charles H. "Sebastien Louis Meurin, S.J." *Illinois Catholic Historical Review* III (1920-1921), 241-59, 371-88; IV (1921-1922), 43-56.

Peterson, Charles E. "Notes on Old Cahokia." *Illinois State Historical Society Journal* XLII (1949), 7-29, 193-208, 313-43.

Peyton, Pauline L. "Pierre Gibault, Priest and Patriot of the Northwest in the Eighteenth Century." *Records of the*

*American Catholic Historical Society of Philadelphia* XII (1901), 452-98.

Pope, A. M. "Father Floquet, the Canadian Friend of the American Patriots." *Records of the American Catholic Historical Society of Philadelphia* V (1888), 63-68, 147-48.

Rothensteiner, John. "Father James Maxwell of Ste. Genevieve." *St. Louis Catholic Historical Review* IV (1922), 142-54.

———— "Historical Sketch of Catholic New Madrid." *St. Louis Catholic Historical Review* IV (1922), 113-29, 206-18.

———— "Paul de Saint Pierre, the First German-American Priest of the West." *Catholic Historical Review* V (1919-1920), 195-222.

Schaaf, Ida M. "The Founding of Sainte Genevieve, Missouri." *Mid-America* XV (1932), 45-49.

Schmitt, Edmond. "The Records of the Parish of St. Francis Xavier at Post Vincennes, Indiana, A.D. 1749-1773." *Records of the American Catholic Historical Society of Philadelphia* XII (1901), 40-60, 193-211, 325-36.

Shaw, Janet P. "Francis Busseron." *Indiana Magazine of History* XXV (1929), 204-15.

Silverberg, Robert. ". . . and the mound builders vanished from the earth." *American Heritage* XX (1969), 60-63, 90-95.

Smith, Sydney F. "The Suppression of the Society of Jesus." *Month* XCIX (1902), 113-31, 263-79, 346-68, 497-517; C (1902), 20-34, 126-52, 258-63, 266-76, 517-36, 581-91.

Storm, Colton. "The Notorious Colonel Wilkins." *Illinois State Historical Society Journal* XL (1947), 7-22.

Thompson, Joseph J. "The Cahokia Mission Property." *Illinois Catholic Historical Review* V (1922-1923), 195-217; VI (1923-1924), 99-135.

———— "Illinois' First Citizen, Pierre Gibault." *Illinois Catholic Historical Review* I (1918-1919), 79-94, 243-48, 380-87, 484-94; II (1919-1920), 85-95; IV (1921-1922), 3-

15, 99-113; V (1922-1923), 226-44; VIII (1925-1926), 3-28, 99-105.

————"Penalties of Patriotism: An Appreciation of the Life, Patriotism and Services of François Vigo, Pierre Gibault, George Rogers Clark and Arthur St. Clair." *Illinois State Historical Society Journal* IX (1917), 401-49.

Walker, Fintan G. "Some Correspondence of an Eighteenth Century Bishop with His Missionaries, 1767-1778." *Catholic Historical Review* XXVII (1941-1942), 186-200.

Wilson, Samuel K. "Bishop Briand and the American Revolution." *Catholic Historical Review* XIX (1933-1934), 129-40.

# INDEX

196

198